They Don't See
What I See

They Don't See What I See

How to Talk with Loved Ones Who Have Crossed Over

Ruth Berger

WEISER BOOKS
San Francisco, CA / Newburyport, MA

First published in 2002 by
Red Wheel/Weiser, LLC
With offices at:
500 Third Street, Suite 230
San Francisco, CA 94107
www.redwheelweiser.com

ISBN-10: 1-57863-263-3
ISBN-13: 978-1-57863-263-3

Library of Congress Cataloging-in-Publication Data
Berger, Ruth.
They don't see what I see : how to talk with loved ones who
have crossed over / Ruth Berger.
p. cm.
ISBN 1-57863-263-3 (pbk.)
1. Spiritualism. 2. Spiritualism—Case studies. 3. Mediums—
Case studies. I. Title.
BF1281 .B35 2002
133.9—dc21
                                        2002008955

Cover image by Patricia Frevert
Cover design by Kathleen Wilson Fivel
Typeset in Sabon

Printed in Canada
TCP
10 9 8 7 6 5 4

Contents

Acknowledgments

Many people have helped me overcome my fears of ghosts during my training and research and I would not have the peace of mind or the understanding of the Other Side without their guidance and support. Dan, my soulmate, who is always at my side offering love and assurance, makes this work possible.

A special thanks to the late Paul Johnson, Robert Ericsson, Marilyn Rossner, Lee Toman, Adella Zunas, Meredith Lady Young, Nan Porter, Rev. Robert Wing, my daughters Karri and Penny, and the many others who taught me how to develop my intuition.

Thanks also to Kelly James-Enger, my writing coach, and to Jill Rogers, my editor, for all their suggestions and encouragement.

Finally I'd like to thank all those people who shared their ghostly experiences with me. Bless you all.

A Note to the Reader

According to a poll taken by the University of Chicago and Andrew Greeley, over 67 percent of people in the United States report having contact with the dead. Fifteen million people claim they've had a near-death experience—and every one of these has lost a loved one. Interest in "life after life" has never been higher.

People want to know what has happened to their loved ones after death. "Is there a message for me?" is the number one question. Guilt, fear, and love are interwoven in their need for information. "Is my loved one all right?" is the second most commonly asked question. Communicating with the Other Side can offer hope and insights—and it can also bring back painful memories. But often peace comes after talking with loved ones in spirit.

You may have already "seen" a ghost or "heard" a noise that couldn't be explained and not told anyone out of fear of sounding odd. Welcome to the world of spirits, ghosts, and other things that go bang in the night.

Listening to ghosts does not mean you are psychotic. You may be hearing voices from the dead because they are asking you to help them. The ghosts from sudden deaths often don't understand what has happened to them. It's not easy having one foot in the spiritual world and the other foot in the physical world. They can need your assistance to move on.

For the past thirty years I've worked with clients as a psychic medium and a medical intuitive and have discovered methods that help people communicate with the spirit world. This book was written to free the mind from negativity and confusion, to help view "life after life" as a natural stage of a constantly changing process.

I used to be afraid of ghosts. Now I'm not. This book is an invitation to explore and experience a greater awareness of life in the hereafter.

So:

Would you like to see a ghost?
What would you want to ask?
Would you be afraid?
Would you trust your senses?

You may find some answers to these questions in the following pages.

(Some names have been changed to protect the privacy of the individuals.)

Chapter 1

Understanding the Unknown

*Just because no one else can see
what you see, does not mean there's
nothing there.*

Have you ever been awakened by an unexplained noise or felt like someone was watching you even though there was no one in the room? You just might have had a ghostly visitor.

Has your child ever called to you in the middle of the night, crying about a monster in the closet? Was he afraid to sleep in his room even after you assured him that you didn't see anything in the closet but his coat? When we don't see what they see or hear what they hear, children get frightened. And just because you can't see what your child sees doesn't necessarily mean there's nothing there. Children see and hear more because they're open psychically.

Carrsen's first word at six months was his grandmother's name. She'd died over a year before. Penny, age four, had conversations at night with her late grandmother. Steve, age three, had an imaginary playmate—his uncle who was dead.

At what age do children who talk to ghosts get labeled as having a mental illness?

Children Who Talk to the Dead: Psychic or Psychotic?

"Go away. You're scaring me," whimpered eleven-year-old Ellen. Her voice was barely audible. She'd been curled up in a ball in the corner of her hospital room for hours. Tears trickled down her face; her eyes were watery and red. "I don't want to see you anymore. You're dead. Leave me alone." No one could hear Ellen because she was speaking inside her mind.

Down the hall, psychiatric nurses Sheila and Nancy were talking. "Ellen worries me," said Sheila. "She says her dead grandfather is trying to take her with him. I don't see him, but Ellen is terrified. What do you think?"

"You worry too much," answered Nancy. "Ellen is a sick child with a very active imagination."

"You're right, but just the same, I'm going to go check on her." Sheila realized that at 3:00 A.M., Ellen would probably be asleep, but she was still worried about the little girl.

She opened the door to Ellen's room quietly and peered into the darkness. At first she couldn't see anything. After her eyes adjusted, she saw Ellen sitting on the floor in the corner, her eyes wide open in terror.

Sheila, a grandmother, automatically reached out and took Ellen into her arms and began to rock her. "Don't be afraid. I'm here. Nothing can hurt you now."

All night Sheila thought about what to do. In the morning she called me. "Can you see me today?" said Sheila. "I read in *Good Housekeeping* that you're a medical intuitive who can talk to ghosts. Can you tell me how to help a terri-fied eleven-year-old girl in our psychiatric ward who says she sees her dead grandfather? The psychiatrist says the best place for this child is in our locked ward, but I disagree. I don't think she's hallucinating. She's a sweet kid and I'm afraid she's going to get worse if she doesn't get help soon."

We set up an emergency appointment for that day. As Sheila walked into my office, I noticed her wrinkled brow and tired eyes. "Tell me about your little girl. I'm going to close my eyes so I can listen intuitively."

As I listened to Sheila's voice, I tuned in and saw the lit-tle girl's face, her terror, and her deceased grandfather stand-ing next to her. I wasn't imagining. The scene was real. After three years of being tested for my psychic abilities at a nearby university, I knew when my intuition was accurate. But I needed more information to go further. "Does the child say why he's there?"

"No. She just starts crying whenever he comes near."

"There are two main reasons why ghosts contact the liv-ing: the first is that the living need them," I explained. "The second is that the dead need the living to do something. My medical intuition tells me that this child and her mother are suffering from mental and physical abuse."

"How do you know that?"

I explained, "I can see a man hitting the child's mother. He's drunk. I see the little girl hiding in her bedroom closet."

Sheila interrupted. "You're right. She used to hide there until her mother said it was safe to come out. What can I do for her?"

"Before I can answer that, I have to find out when the first incident occurred.

"I see the child at six months waking up to loud voices. She doesn't like the sounds. She cries for comfort, but no one comes. That was the first time her grandfather came to her. She wasn't old enough to realize he was dead and she allowed his spirit energy to soothe her. She fell asleep. He kept coming until she told her mother about his visits. Her mother got afraid and told her to never let him return. The child trusted her mother and stopped being comforted by the grandfather, which was a big loss for her. The child needs to trust what she sees. At some level, her grandfather is real. Denying what she sees is creating tremendous fear.

"You can help her by asking her questions," I continued. "What does he look like? Is his face kind? What is he wearing? Tell the child to say 'I love you' to her grandfather. That will distract her enough to be able to hear what he has to say. Hold her hand so she won't be afraid. Then tell her to ask him what he wants. Try to understand and don't be frightened. Respond with your love and common sense. Once she gets the message, she'll be able to sleep and she'll get better."

"I'm not sure I can remember it all. Can I call you if I need more help?"

"Of course."

A week later Sheila called. "I did what you recommended and the child responded beautifully. I feel she's got a built-in helper now and I've become a believer in ghosts. Bless you."

***

Often I get calls from medical aides, nurses, paramedics, and psychologists who have hunches or feelings about a patient. They don't necessarily believe in psychics or medical intuitives, but their desperation leads them to call me.

Children often see ghosts that adults cannot and they get scared when people in authority do not see the ghosts or understand what to do to help them. Some doctors call ghost visits hallucinations and prescribe Prozac or Ritalin to stop the child's visions. They don't realize that tranquilizing the child makes it easier for ghosts to be seen and heard. The child can't see or hear ghosts when their minds are busy thinking about sports, schoolwork, and friends.

I've Been There

I remember being awakened when I was fifteen by a gray cloud pouring through my closet door toward me. The cloud became larger and thicker until I could see the forms of two robed men coming closer and closer. I pulled the blanket over my head, but I couldn't breathe. I screamed, "Ma, Pa! Help! They're back again!"

"Not again," my father hollered as he flipped on the light, threw open the closet door, and checked under my bed. "You're too old to be frightened of the night. Anyway, there's no one here. Now go back to sleep." He shut off the light and went back to bed.

Quietly I shut my bedroom door and turned the light back on. I had learned that as long as the lights were on, they wouldn't come back. I didn't know who I was more afraid of—the two strangers whom no one else could see, my father's temper, or my mother making fun of me to my brothers at breakfast.

My family didn't believe me. I couldn't tell my friends for fear they'd make fun of me too. Was I imagining the two men? Why couldn't anyone else see them? Who were they? What did they want?

I wanted to sleep through the night and stop fearing the unknown. I wanted to be normal. Twelve months of these two men waking me up every night was making me wonder if I was losing my mind.

One morning I woke up rested. I'd slept through the night. No one had awakened me. Excited, I wondered whether it was possible that the two men had left. The second night went by without interruption. Then the third and fourth night, I began to feel optimistic. After two months had passed without a visit from the night visitors, I stopped counting. They were gone—forever, I hoped. Would they return? I prayed they wouldn't.

How different my life would be today if I'd known then what I know now! I might have listened to the ghosts and found answers. Maybe I wouldn't have been so afraid.

Years later I heard my four-year-old daughter talking to someone in her room at night. I went in and asked who she was speaking with.

"Grandma," she said to me. "She comes every night."

My throat tightened and my eyes flooded with tears. I was terrified, and I didn't think I believed in life after life. I took her arm and said to her, "Your grandmother is dead. She can't talk to you or anyone else. This is all imaginary, so stop it." When I left her room I was shaking. I remember leaning against the wall in the hall outside her door. Through the closed door I heard her say, "Shhh. Mommy's afraid. I'm not. We'll just talk quieter."

Penny wasn't afraid of ghosts. She continued to demonstrate her psychic skills and opened the door for me to learn about my own intuitive abilities. My child became my teacher.

Beyond Chance

"How could my eleven-year-old daughter, Penny, pick 99 percent of the Academy Award winners?" I asked my coworker Jenny. "The only time she missed was when she wanted her favorite star to win."

Jenny, an intelligent, beautiful, slim woman who never appeared to get riled in a crisis, responded eagerly. "Your daughter is psychic," she said. "Intuition works best when desire and greed get out of the way.

"I've noticed you've been studying graphology and 'seeing' into the future," she continued. "Handwriting analysis shows personality tendencies, not what will happen tomorrow or the day after. If you're interested in psychic phenomena, I'll bring you a book you may want to read."

Positive she was wrong about the purpose of graphology, I reread every page of my $.50 book on the subject. She was right.

The next day Jenny brought me a book about psychic phenomena and placed it on my desk. I read the entire book that night, unable to put it down. For the first time I had an idea of what had been happening to me all my life. In high school, I'd been the resident "Ann Landers." My friends would ask me questions about their love lives and test scores and I'd give them the answers. My classmates had never helped me the same way so I thought they didn't care. But when I'd read this book, a light went on in my head. I realized they hadn't been able to see what I saw. I hadn't realized how psychic I was. I got excited. I wanted to learn more. When my friend asked me to join a study group, I didn't hesitate.

Understanding Sets the Foundation

The weekly sessions with the study group filled my mind and body with love and understanding. I was accepted and encouraged to talk about my strange experiences here. In this group of women, finally, I could be me.

For the first time I met people who also had unexplained occurrences and talked about them without fear of ridicule. I felt safe among these women, my soul sisters, who wouldn't want to lock me up because I saw things they didn't. No one criticized or laughed at me.

We talked about everything: our fears, dreams, tastes, goals, relationships, and desires. There were never any put-downs or negative responses to my questions, only intuitive insights on how to accomplish what was needed or wanted. No subject was taboo.

We were encouraged to meditate to enhance our connection to the earthly world and the spirit world. My intuition expanded so rapidly that often I couldn't tell when I was using my intuition or when I was being logical. The support of the group kept me from falling off the cliff of sanity.

Whenever I was afraid, they gave me unconditional love. When something would happen that didn't make sense, they'd help me understand how to use my intuition to get past my confusion. Slowly, I learned to trust my intuition more fully, and with that trust, came accuracy. During the next two years I read every book I could find on the paranormal. I couldn't get information fast enough.

All my life I'd been plagued by an eating problem. When someone talked about something during a meal, I would "see" what they were talking about on my plate. Discussions of surgery made my meat take on the appearance of blood and guts. Conversations about the flu or vomiting would cause me to leave the table without eating.

Reading books about intuition helped me understand why I suffered so much when people talked about these things during meals. I hadn't realized how sensitive I was and how simply mentioning something would automatically make me visualize what was being said. At least it helped me stay thin for years!

The more I learned, the more I understood. The more I understood, the more I let go of the pain of being different.

Saved from Poverty by Her Father's Spirit

A group member asked me to do a psychic reading for one of her friends, a woman I'd never met before named Mary. I reluctantly agreed to go to Mary's home and give her an ESP consultation.

As soon as Mary answered the door I said, "Your husband has a message for you." I don't know why I said it, and I repeated the words again even after she said, "He's been dead for over twenty-five years."

Why was I saying I had a message from a man who had been dead for twenty-five years? The next few words that came out of my mouth were even more bizarre.

"Your husband wants you to believe he's here," I replied. "He says the book with his favorite poem is still on the end table next to your bed." I couldn't see her bedroom. How did I know about the book? I was scared. What was going on?

Mary smiled and said, "That book is still there. I read it often, especially his favorite poem."

I heard myself ask, "Do you have a candle? It's easier to see spirits when the lights are not so bright."

She went looking for a candle while I waited in the kitchen, half wanting to bolt out of the house. This experience was becoming more than I thought I could handle.

Mary returned with the candle and shut off all the electric lights. Suddenly my voice burst out, "Don't let our daughter sign the papers tomorrow." I didn't understand what was happening. Who was this daughter?

As if Mary could read my mind, she replied, "Our only child lives in California. She's been going through a messy divorce. I'll call her as soon as we're done and give her the message."

Bewildered, I questioned silently, "What was I doing here?"

During the next hour I repeated his words again and again. "Don't let our daughter sign the papers tomorrow." What papers? I had no idea what was happening and didn't want to know. I just wanted the evening to end. Thankfully, we finished and I went home.

The phone was ringing when I arrived at my house. Mary had immediately called her daughter in California but her daughter didn't know what this "message" was about. I was relieved. Now I could just write the experience off as a figment of my imagination.

The next morning, Mary called again. "I just got off the phone with my daughter. She forgot about an appointment she had with her lawyer this afternoon. She's been dating him for over a month. She doesn't think there's anything to worry about but, just in case, I warned her not to sign anything."

I returned home from my secretary's job at 5:00 P.M. to find a message on my answering machine. Mary wanted me to call her as soon as I could.

My hand shook as I dialed the number. "My husband was right," she said. "The papers that Suzy's lawyer wanted her to sign were her divorce papers relinquishing all financial obligation from her soon-to-be ex-husband. California law dictates that all monetary assets be divided 50/50. Suzy's been dating the attorney so she trusted him and would have signed the papers without reading them. Her husband had set the whole thing up. My daughter and her four children would have been left with nothing! I'm so glad you were able to give me my husband's message. We can't thank you enough."

I was glad for Mary's daughter, but I didn't want to talk to her husband again, no matter what the reason. But several days later, Mary's husband suddenly appeared in my car as I was driving to work. He wanted me to call Mary and tell her Suzy wanted to commit suicide. I told him there was no way I could tell Mary that her daughter, who was 3,000 miles away, was about to kill herself.

"Tell her," he yelled and jabbed my shoulder so hard I swerved and almost had an accident. "You've got to save my daughter."

"Okay, but on one condition: that you never come see me again." He agreed.

I didn't actually call Mary. I had just said I would to get her husband out of the car. But later that afternoon, Mary phoned and asked if I had a message for her. My head felt like a hammer was hitting it straight down the middle.

"Yes," I answered, "call your daughter. Your husband says she's depressed."

An hour later, Mary called again and said, "I am so grateful. If I hadn't called my daughter, she said she would have killed herself."

Mary's husband kept his word. I never saw him again. Without her father's intervention through me, Suzy would have been broke. She didn't know about the attorney's deception and neither did her mother. I wasn't mind reading, or storytelling. I hadn't imagined Mary's husband in the car with me. His message was factual.

Trusting the Healing Process

After I got divorced in 1968, I made a steadfast resolution to trust my instincts and not blindly accept what others told me. I walked out of the past and into the future.

I soon met a man who was open to all aspects of the mind but grounded in science. Dan gave me unconditional love and neither encouraged nor discouraged my imagination. He became my rock and my husband.

My study group was teaching me that using my intuition was normal. They were not afraid of what I saw and heard intuitively. They showered me with unconditional love and accepted all of the strange experiences I related to them.

I'd had ghost visitations all my life but the people who were closest to me didn't see or understand what was happening. Until I met people who could help me understand what was happening, I was lost in a sea of despair. My new friends and mentor taught me the beginning levels of "medical intuition"; not to be afraid, not to doubt, and most of all, how to heal the wounds of myself and others.

My interaction with these people helped build the foundation for my ghost training. I became more accurate intuitively but my biggest training came in 1975 when I was diagnosed with advanced emphysema and was told that my condition would only get worse. I went from doctor to doctor in search of help, but no one gave me any hope or even believed that I'd never smoked.

I got progressively worse and had to carry an oxygen tank with me everywhere I went. It wasn't until a psychic did a medical intuition session on me, and told me what type of doctor to look for and what to say, that I got help I needed and eventually recovered.

The holistic doctor I found had me learn yoga, do breathing exercises, change my diet, and focus on wellness. My intuitive training helped me meditate on his suggestions. With his and my group's help, I was able to discover and discard old habits and cure myself.

Now I help people learn how to intuitively x-ray the body to find the primary reason for an ailment, discover how past lives affect our health, and develop a path for wellness.

Unexpected Events
Are Learning Experiences

Our weekly group session always began with reports of any unusual phenomena that occurred over the previous seven days.

"My week began when I was buying some makeup and said 'Happy Birthday' to the clerk," I reported. "I didn't know her and wasn't even thinking about her. What scared me was her response—she said, 'Thank you, but *how* did you know?' How *did* I know?"

The leader responded, "You keep testing yourself, that's good."

At that same meeting, another member reported, "I have a reoccurring dream that always foretells the death of someone close. I had that dream this week and three days later, my uncle died. I hate that dream!"

This reminded me of a similar experience I had had when I was fourteen, which I described to the group. I had been in my bedroom when I heard a man's voice say, "Your grandmother's going to die today." My grandmother had been dying for two years and we'd had many scares, but nothing like this had ever happened, I had never heard a voice telling me my grandmother was going to die. I ran to her room. She was sitting up eating breakfast. Nothing made sense.

I went back to my bedroom to get dressed for school and heard the voice say again, but this time even louder, "Your grandmother's going to die today." I remember asking, "Who are you? Why are you trying to scare me?" But I didn't get an answer. I kept stalling and didn't want to leave the house, but my mother sent me off to school.

As soon as my classes were over, I phoned home. My mother told me a lie. She'd said everything was okay. But it wasn't. My grandmother had died shortly after I'd left for school.

Whose voice had I heard? Why did I get the message and not my mother? Why didn't anyone else hear the voice? Knowing something can be terrifying, especially when you don't know how you got the information.

Finding My Spiritual Teacher

I often wondered why I always agreed to get involved in unknown situations. TV minister Rev. Robert Schuller says, "People who say yes before knowing the outcome are possibility thinkers." If that's true, I must be one of the greatest possibility thinkers in the world.

Saying yes has brought me closer to God because after I said yes, all I wanted to do was pray. I said yes to doing a psychic standup show before I knew what I was getting into. I said yes to being a guinea pig for scientists interested in investigating the paranormal. Each time I said yes, my world expanded.

Barely a year had passed since I'd begun to formally study ESP with my group. How I wish my life could have been different. I envied my friend Muriel whose family understood her ghosts. She couldn't understand my family's rejection of what I saw.

Why had it taken me so long to get help? Why was my family so hard on me? I was only a child. Was I lucky that I wasn't put in a locked ward in a hospital and given medicines or unlucky because I didn't get medical assistance? There was no psychiatric nurse to help me. One of the study group members told me, "You were like an oyster with a pearl inside. You grew from the irritation. Friction makes the jewel."

One day, another group member called to tell me about an upcoming conference on the paranormal. She gave me a phone number where I could get information. I wasn't feeling well, in fact, I'd had a fever of 103 degrees for several days but I called anyway.

A man who introduced himself as Paul Johnson answered the phone. When I started speaking, he said, "You sound awful. Come to my office and I'll channel a healing for your throat."

"Are you a doctor?"

"No, a faith healer."

I wondered if I could trust this person who I'd never met before? But I was sick and felt I had nothing to lose. I went to see him and he had me sit in a chair while he placed his large hands on my hot forehead. Instantly, my head cooled down and my throat stopped hurting. "How did you do that?"

"I've been studying faith healing for many years." He explained. "Now I'm the President, organizer, and cofounder of Spiritual Advisory Council, an educational group that teaches healing, psychic phenomena, and spirit communication."

I had found my spiritual teacher.

My First Séance

My psychic training was going great until one day the leader announced, "Next week we're going to try to communicate with people who have died."

Terror struck. My head started to pound and my body shook. I wanted no part of this. I held my head in my hands.

"Ruth, there's nothing to be afraid of," she said. "We'll keep the lights on. Dead people can't hurt you."

Keep the lights on! Dead people! Ghosts! Chills went through me. What if one of them took control of my mind? What if I had a heart attack during the séance? The what-ifs tormented me for the entire seven days before the séance.

My legs were rubbery when I walked into the house where the séance was going to be held.

I sat next to a young man on a long, blue silk couch. His hazel-colored eyes looked as frightened as I felt. His voice quivered as he asked, "Is this your first séance?" I nodded yes with tears in my eyes.

He saw my fright and took command. "I'm afraid too. Don't worry. We'll probably laugh about this later."

What a kind man. I felt safer knowing we were both inexperienced and frightened. I prayed that as long as we were together, nothing bad would happen.

Listening to our leader's soothing voice guide us into meditation helped me release my fears and relax. I was in such a peaceful place that when I heard my mother's voice at first I didn't remember that she'd died five years earlier.

Then, all at once, I remembered. This couldn't be my mother speaking. She was dead. I opened my eyes and looked around. Everyone else's eyes were closed. Then I heard her broken English again. Her voice was coming from Bob, the young man sitting next to me.

"Ruthie, you vork too hard. You're not eating right." It was true. I hadn't changed! Was it possible my mother was alive at some level and could speak to me?

The young man jerked his shoulders and opened his eyes. "I don't like this," he said.

"Don't stop," I begged him. "You sound just like my mother. Do it again."

"No way. This is too freaky," he said, but he didn't move. Later, he told me he couldn't stand up because his legs were too weak.

My voice had disturbed the others. The leader suggested we take a break, change partners, and continue meditating. I was too excited to relax.

Again I heard my mother's voice coming through my new partner's mouth, two more partners, two more messages telling me to take it easy, rest more. "Ruthie, you vork too hard, you don't eat right." It was always the same message. I thought, she'd always been a nag. But my curiosity was piqued. I wanted more.

It's been almost thirty years since my first connection with my mother' spirit. After hundreds of séances, she's still giving the same message today. Some things never change.

Can the dead speak? Yes, but you may not want to hear what they have to say.

Evil Energy Followed Me Home

The university research team had been called to investigate a family that reported an unexplained psychic phenomena. They invited me to go with them to "tune in" and report anything I heard, saw, or felt. The opportunity excited me. If I'd known what lay ahead, I wouldn't have been so eager.

We went to a small house in a northwest suburb of Chicago. The only information I'd been given was that a fifteen-year-old girl was having nightmares and waking up with unexplained bites on her throat.

Once inside the house, we were all led upstairs to the daughter's bedroom where the alleged biting took place. I entered the room and instantly felt a vice pressing tightly on both sides of my forehead. The slanted ceiling above her bed was breathing. Fascinated but cautious, I moved slowly closer to explore. My heart began to beat so loudly I was sure everyone could hear it. My lungs closed and tears filled my eyes. Evil lurked in this room. I knew it. I heard one of the parapsychologists calling, "Are you okay? Are you having an asthma attack?"

I pointed to the ceiling. "It's breathing. Can't you see it?" The group pushed past me in their eagerness to have a psychic experience. Their hands touched the place that was breathing but they didn't feel or see anything.

"Touch the area on the ceiling over the pillow." I whispered. No one had the same reaction as me. The research group saw my face turn pale white and they were afraid I was going to faint. I plopped down on a chair by the door but suddenly I had to get out of this room. I jumped up and ran down the stairs, yelling, "We have to get rid of this evil. We've got to go downstairs right now and meditate."

I had no idea what I was going to do. I trusted my instincts like an animal in danger. I asked that the front door be opened and that everyone sit in a circle holding hands while chanting "God is here. God is here. God is here."

I heard a terrible noise and turned just in time to see a dark horrible monster shape with ugly, beaded eyes rushing down the stairs and out the front door. It wasn't human. No one else saw the ugly image leave but I was deeply relieved to have it gone.

After it left, I was able to breathe freely again. Never in my life had I been so terrified. I was surprised I didn't have a heart attack. The next hour was a blur to me. I listened as the research team asked questions of the inhabitants of the house. All I wanted to do was go home to bed. My body and mind were exhausted.

As my husband and I walked back to our car, I saw the ugly presence sneering at me from the backseat. I stopped and looked at my husband. He was unaware of the monster. Was I crazy? Was I imagining the whole thing? I didn't tell my husband for fear he'd want to lock me up. Instead I asked him to take me to a bar for a drink.

"You don't drink," he said puzzled.

"Take me to a bar," I repeated without explaining.

He'd lived with me long enough to realize I was serious. We drove to a restaurant with a bar. My plan was to stay there long enough for the evil presence to get bored and leave. Two hours and one drink later, he was still in the backseat, grinning. I prayed for him to please go away. He didn't. For the next two months the entity sat in the corner of our bedroom. I couldn't sleep for more than an hour at a time, terrified that he would take over my body. I was afraid to tell anyone. Fear consumed me night and day.

One evening I saw the evil presence at my study group. Unable to hold back any longer, I burst out crying and told the group all about it. Instead of ridicule and disbelief, they offered support. The leader said, "We've got to help Ruth rid herself of this evil. Ruth, repeat my words in a strong, firm voice, 'You are no longer welcome.'"

I repeated the words but my voice shook.

"Say the words louder," she instructed. "Speak up. He has no right to be in your home."

"You have no right to be in my home," I repeated after her.

"You must leave now. God is here." As I said the words, the evil presence began to fade. This gave me courage. "Get out and don't come back," I said boldly. To my sheer amazement, he left and never returned.

"Could it be that simple?" I asked.

"Yes," the leader said. "Next time, don't wait. Tell us right away."

"Yes, I promise." Free at last! Relief flowed as I realized I could have saved myself a lot of stress if I had told them sooner.

Scary ghosts are like uninvited guests. They come when they want and leave when you tell them to. The spirit's will wasn't stronger than mine. The monster was just a bully.

When I stood up to him, he wilted. Letting go of my psychic fears helped me have more faith.

Deepening My Spiritual Awareness

I was hungry to experience the spiritual path, to be more aware of the spirit connection and to learn how to help people and myself. I wanted to delve deeper into the trance connection. The fear of channeling was no longer blocking me. At our weekly meditation group, my confidence grew as I observed Paul's trust in his own trance development as he received messages from spirits.

During the months that followed, I'd wake and journal my dreams and thoughts on my computer. Then I'd surround myself with light and ask God for any insights for the day. Afterward, I'd ask for healing guidance for loved ones and clients.

Psychic Vampirism

"There are three levels of intuition," the group leader once explained to me. "The receiver, the sender, and the combination of the two. You are a receiver. You get psychic information but often you don't know when the information is yours or someone else's. I think people have been draining your energy with their fears for years. I've got a book on psychic vampirism that I think you should read."

After reading the book, I knew the leader was right. For the first time I could see how easy it was for people to send their negative thoughts into my energy field or aura.

After the next group meditation, another member said excitedly, "Ruth, I know why you have such a hard time letting go of your fears. You don't know how to let go of other people's stuff. During our meditation, I had a vision of you visualizing a white light washing over your body whenever you feel afraid. Why don't you try it now?"

Her aura was wide and bright, and I trusted her but I still felt strange closing my eyes while the rest of the group watched me. I'd always been shy but I realized the fastest way to get this over with was to just do it. I began to imagine white energy flowing quickly through my body, and my anxiety faded. I wondered if someone had done something psychic to me and my fears returned in abundance.

Another member said, "I feel your fears heavy on my chest. Exhale. You're holding your breath."

I exhaled and felt my body relax. For the first time in my life, people knew what I needed without me verbally asking them. Now I realized I was a receiver as well as a sender.

Developing Trust in Healing Spirits

A few days later, terror struck as I was watching TV. My mind kept dwelling on one of my friend's fears of never finding the right life partner. My body hurt. I walked around in a daze praying, "Lord help me. I think I'm going mad."

I heard a male voice say, "Relax. Lie down. Visualize white energy flowing through you. Remember how it has helped you in the past. Let go of all other thoughts." The voice continued. "Now imagine your friend flooded with white light energy. Say the words 'all is well' aloud as if she could hear you. Then bless her and yourself. When you're finished, visualize her image fading out of your mind."

I felt like a fifty-pound weight had been lifted from my chest and my head stopped hurting as soon as the vision vanished.

"Let your light grow brighter and remember to bask in the light whenever you feel afraid."

Another voice asked, "Do you feel better?" I nodded. My body felt calm but I was mystified. At the next meeting, I related my experience.

The leader responded immediately, "It sounds like you have a spirit guiding you through an episode of energy vampirism. Even though she was far away, you absorbed your friend's fears into yourself. This lesson is a reminder for you to do the white light exercise whenever you feel afraid, and to keep doing it until the fear dissipates." Then the leader asked if I had ever heard the voice before. I realized that I had, that it was the same voice that I had heard when I was fourteen.

Psychometry and the Healing Group

Psychometry is a technique for finding out information about a person by touching or holding an object belonging to that individual. Because people often leave energy "imprints" on things they wear, a sensitive person can pick up these energies from the object and discover a great deal about the one who wore it.

Our leader said, "Tonight's exercise will require you to take off your watches and pass them to the member on your right. Place the watch in your left palm and cover it with your right hand. Close your eyes and notice what you feel."

The watch I was holding felt sharp and cold. Like a shot, I dropped it on the table.

"Hey, why did you put my watch down so fast?"

I was afraid to tell the woman what I felt. The leader placed her hand gently on my shoulder. Softly she said, "This is a study group doing research. Just say whatever you felt. Don't hold back."

I started to cry. My chest hurt. No one had ever understood how emotional I got when other people were hurting.

I sobbed aloud, "You're worried about your mother. You think she's going to die."

"Keep talking," said the member as her eyes flooded with tears. The last thing I wanted to do was talk, but she looked so sad. I closed my eyes and spoke the words I heard in my head, "Don't be afraid, your mother needs surgery, but she'll be fine."

"You're right. My mother's going to have a gallbladder operation in the morning," said the member. "I've been terrified that she might have cancer."

Validation! The pain in my chest faded. Without any forethought, I asked, "Have you been having pains in your chest?"

"Yes," she answered. "I wondered if I was having a gallbladder problem too."

"No, you're fine. You're just absorbing your mother's symptoms like some men do when their wives are pregnant." She laughed and so did the others.

The leader asked, "Ruth, did you know any of this before the meditation?"

The other member responded angrily, "Why are you doubting Ruth? I only found out about the surgery a few hours ago. I came tonight to ask the group to pray for my mother."

"I'm sorry," the leader continued, "but I had to be sure Ruth hadn't picked up the information beforehand. How did you get this information?"

I tried hard to remember. Slowly I said, "When I first held her watch, I felt pressure and pain in my chest. The problems lessened when I got rid of the watch, but returned when she asked a question. Her prodding forced me to come up with something. I thought I was imagining her mother being sick. Then, I just talked without thinking. Until she confirmed the message, I thought I had made it all up.

"I heard a male voice, strong and firm telling me all would go well. He sounded so loving, I felt relieved. I think I just used my common sense. All my pains left when I gave her the message."

"Was the voice you heard the same one who told you your grandmother was going to die?" asked the leader.

"I don't know and I don't want to find out."

The leader said, "Trust me. You need to find out who is speaking. Close your eyes and ask who spoke."

My heart began to pound but I followed her instructions. I asked silently for the information. "I am Dr. John and I am the leader of the Healing Group," said the voice I'd heard in my head. "You are going to be a great healer. We are here to help you." My heart stopped racing. "There are six of us at present. We represent the colors of your world. I am Caucasian and represent the medical world. Adrienne is from Venus and represents love. Ari is a black man from Africa who represents courage. Dr. Wu is a Chinese philosopher. The Redman represents nature. Ragu is a Tibetan Lama."

I told the group what I'd heard and they were happy for me. All my life I'd been an introvert, afraid to say the wrong things, to laugh out loud, and to look foolish. The psychic group didn't make fun of me or my strange ideas.

Nothing would ever be the same again. Like a log being propelled rapidly down a river stream, I was being led into the ghostly dimension.

Steps to See What I See

1. You can use the following questions to help access your own intuitive experiences.

    *   Have you ever seen someone that no one else saw?
    *   How old were you?
    *   Were you afraid?
    *   How did others react?
    *   Write as fully as you can about your experience.

2. Read books about ghost experiences.
3. Find a support group that believes in ghosts.
4. Seek out classes/workshops that support you spiritually.

Chapter 2

Creating an Intuitive Pathway

*The real voyage of discovery consists
not in seeing new landscapes, but in
having new eyes.*
—Marcel Proust

Beginning the Adventure

The more I learned, the more I wanted to experience. Every
time my husband and I walked past a particular restaurant,
I'd have a sense that someday I was going to do psychic readings there.

One day I followed my hunch and went in to talk to the
owner. He hired me on one condition—I couldn't turn anyone away. There was a large bar in the front of the restaurant and I was worried that someone who was drunk might
request a reading. Drunks scared me. They smelled bad and
were unpredictable. But the owner said that I either had to
read for anyone who asked or I wouldn't be able to work
there. A higher force must have been watching over me

because in the three years I worked there, no one who was drunk ever asked for a reading.

The restaurant was noisy, but I enjoyed challenging my intuition. How much could I see? How much could I speak of what I saw? I started setting morals for the intuitive information I gave out.

One woman wanted to know if her adult daughter was having sex with her boyfriend. I didn't think it was any of the mother's business and told her that I couldn't see anything.

Another woman asked if her husband was cheating on her. Her aura was so dark. When I asked my higher mind what would happen if I told her the truth, the answer came back that she would kill herself. I told her I didn't know the answer to her question. I prayed for the woman and a week later, she returned. We talked for a long time. She was ready for the truth. We became good friends and I never regretted waiting to tell her what she wanted to know.

My goals for a good reading are:

1. to have the client leave my office feeling better
2. to give accurate information
3. to "tune in" to the lesson the client needs to learn
4. to be kind
5. to do no harm
6. to offer information that empowers the client
7. to give alternative solutions on how their lives can improve

Picture This!

One evening, the group leader asked us to bring in photographs of family and friends. We were encouraged to verbalize any intuitive impressions we received when we looked at the photos.

I felt nothing intuitively at first. The others in the group had many impressions. One knew that the person in the photo had died. Another could tell that the man in the photo had just recovered from cancer. It turned out that it had been a year since his last radiation treatment. Another could tell that the girl in the photo had moved out of the state a year ago. All the information was confirmed.

I learned that looking at a photo opened my intuitive mind. At first I was only aware of the physical appearance of the person; age, coloring, and whether their expressions were happy or sad. All left-brain input. As I would focus on the photos, my energy field and emotions would merge with the person in the photo. Sometimes I'd become hesitant, unsure, anxious, and begin to suffer the same feelings the individual in the photo was suffering.

I learned that my senses were processing too much information that may not be important. I learned to think like a detective, asking myself questions like, Why am I getting this feeling? What is happening to this person? In the groups, we were instructed not to analyze or jump ahead to logical explanations, but to first let our imaginations run wild and ask our intuition what to do.

With patience, the right answer often came like a light-bulb going on in my head or like the "ah ha" feeling in my stomach. Over the years, our group experimented with photographs many times. Little by little, I began to do better. Now it's my favorite way to tune in.

Imagination Frames Events Unknown

Often, I couldn't make any sense of the messages I gave at the weekly sessions, but with the leader's encouragement, I began to verbalize my impressions. The process was fascinating when I allowed my intuition to guide me. More details would become clear. Meditation also helped me to understand the different levels of mind consciousness.

Could our brain work at a higher level by using our intuition more?

Why do people stifle their imagination?

What are they afraid of?

Seeing Auras
Increases Intuitive Accuracy

I first saw halos around people's heads at the age of three. If the person's halo was bright and more than two inches wide, I'd feel fine. If the halo or aura was dark and thin, I'd get a sick feeling in my stomach. In my childhood, people with dirty auras would often pat my head and say things like, "Isn't she sweet?" Yuck! I hated that word and would even have nasty thoughts about people who had dirty auras. I'd learned that when someone's aura was filled with dirty spots, I'd have to pray hard to protect myself from taking on too much of that person's negative energy.

My fellow group members were fascinated by my experiences with auras. They wanted to know if everyone could see the human aura. I thought about the question for a while and then began to explain what I understood. I explained that anyone can see auras, but that you don't see them with your eyes. You feel them first with your heart, or your senses. Then as you concentrate, you can become aware of colors around people's heads, which are their auras shining forth.

The leader asked me if I could teach the others how to see the energy field. In a way, her question surprised me as I had assumed that everyone saw auras. I wondered why they didn't, to me it seemed so natural. It also caught me off guard that she thought I could help the group. They'd been studying ESP for over twenty years. I was the newcomer.

I suggested to the group that they close their eyes and imagine the color they see when they're with a person they love.

"I saw pink," one member said, "but isn't that my imagination working overtime?"

"In the beginning, you'll think you're imagining the auras," I answered. "With practice, you'll see the aura with your mind."

Another member said, "I didn't get a color when I saw my son. I just saw darkness."

"Are you having problems with your son?" I asked.

Her face turned crimson. "Yes, but how did you know?"

"I saw darkness in your head spreading and touching your heart," I said. "I heard a voice saying that your son has been giving you a hard time lately."

"Can we change the subject please?"

To spare her more embarrassment, I said, "That's all I heard." She and I both knew there was more. Part of being intuitive is knowing when to stop.

"Is it always bad news when you see darkness in the aura?" another member asked.

"Most of the time, but not all the time. Sometimes darkness in the aura is caused by a false fear, like fearing the dentist, but knowing the dentist is really there to help you."

"I became frightened when I saw darkness around my husband," she explained.

I checked out her aura and saw darkness at the back of her head. I wondered what that meant so I closed my eyes to "tune in." Immediately I saw people being led to the arena to face the lions. The vision was so clear. I could hear the hungry animals and the crying of the victims. I saw the member who had asked the question kneeling in prayer next to another woman. Never before had I seen a past life so clearly. I began to describe what I was seeing aloud.

"In a past life you and your sister then, your husband now, were killed by lions because you wouldn't renounce your religion," I said. "You were the leader and your sister died because you were so stubborn. Now you worry that your husband will die because of you."

The woman gasped as tears came streaming down her face. "That's my worst fear! Will he die because of me? I couldn't handle it."

"No, he won't." I'd closed my eyes again and imagined thirty years into the future. "I see you both healthy and living together well into your nineties." I opened my eyes and saw tears flowing from most of the members' eyes. The room was filling with white light. I realized a healing had taken place.

"You did well, Ruth," said the leader. "Thank you. I could see her aura shining brightly."

Why didn't everyone see what I saw?

Why were people afraid of their intuition?

Why didn't they trust their instincts?

Why hadn't I?

I pondered how child prodigies could play a musical instrument without any prior training or how Alexander Graham Bell invented the telephone or how Thomas Edison developed power transmission facilities. I read about Dr. Carl Jung, psychologist, who believed in a Universal Intelligence that everyone could tap in to to get any and all answers to life's questions.

Was that what I was doing?

Intuition Testing Is Fun

Call me weird, call me crazy. When a local university advertised for intuitives for a research program, I signed up. I wanted to learn more about how my intuition worked and how accurate I really was. After three years of testing, my intuition was found to be between 85–92 percent accurate.

Card tests left me cold. The researcher would shuffle a deck of cards, turn up one card at a time facing away from me. I had to guess which card he was looking at and then which card he would turn over next.

I didn't often get the card the other person was looking at, which tested my mind-reading skills, but I did score above average when predicting the card that came next, a test for clairvoyant abilities. Another test featured a high screen with a black fabric sleeve that I put my hand through. I was to try and guess which color I was touching. Here again, I scored higher than average when intuiting which color could be next.

The fourth test had me trying to "tune in" to a person in another room. The other person was given a photograph to focus on while I "tuned" in to his or her thoughts and described what he was thinking. I did fairly well on this test.

My best results though came through psychometry testing; holding a piece of jewelry or handwriting sample in my left hand and "seeing," intuitively, what the person looked like. I couldn't just say brown for hair or eye color. The test required me to be more specific. Height had to be within three inches and weight within five pounds.

I remember holding a greeting card and "seeing" a blind man searching for his wife and child. My distant viewing showed me where the wife had gone and how her husband could get in touch with her. I scored 100 percent on this test.

I still enjoy testing myself by trying to guess which of the three elevators in an office building will come first, what the weather will be like in seven days, and tuning in before a meeting with a client to know what they will ask.

I Became a Standup Psychic

My professional career as a standup psychic began when I agreed to do mini readings for a national charity group. I thought it would give me an opportunity to test and stretch my intuitive skills. I assumed all I had to do was sit in a corner and read for a few people. Was I ever wrong!

When I got to the meeting place, there were eighty people sitting theater-style waiting to hear what I had to say. Panic set in. What if my intuition failed? What if my mind went blank? Or I fainted from fright? During the show, a spirit stood in front of me while I was talking to a woman in the audience. The spirit kept blocking me, insisting he had a message for the woman I was talking to.

Unable to get past the messenger, I gave in and told the woman her deceased husband had a message. The audience gasped. I heard whispers. "How did she know her husband was dead?"

I said, "Your husband says the money you need is in the bank. He says to look in his old summer jacket to find the information and key for the box." The woman began to sob.

After the show, the widow stopped me as I was leaving. "I never believed in ESP or ghosts," she said, "but as soon as I get home, I'm going to look for the key. I've been searching for it since my husband died a year ago. I never thought to look in his jacket. Thank you."

As she turned away, I saw her wiping her eyes with tissue. Part of me was happy the woman would be helped. The other part of me wondered what was happening. The next day she called to say she'd found the key where her husband had told her to look.

What if I hadn't followed through? Would she have found the key anyway? I didn't like ghosts interrupting me. I wanted to be in control.

Every time I did a show, I got requests for private consultations. I never thought I'd be a psychic when I grew up, but suddenly I was thrust in the role with only one way to go—forward!

My psychic work accelerated. Another year went by swiftly and my intuition flowed more easily and more accurately than ever before. I became known for my humor and speed. I could give forty "mini" psychic readings in less than forty-five minutes. People began comparing me to a combination of Dr. Ruth and Lily Tomlin.

My goals for a show were to have fun and be accurate while demonstrating the many dimensions of the psychic mind—past lives, future options, and ways to heal. I'd ask individuals to stand up to ask questions. When they stood up, I could separate their auras from the others who were sitting near them, and hear only one person's voice at a time. Before they finished, I'd have the answer, and would speak swiftly and accurately—often causing the audience to roar with delight at the shocked response of the questioner.

At one demonstration, a woman of ninety asked me to tell her anything I saw intuitively. I said, "You're going to find the love of your life soon." She almost fell into her chair shocked. Thirty seconds later, she stood up again and asked, "Will he be rich?" The audience laughed for almost three minutes. People liked trying to second-guess what I'd say.

My response was instant and joyful unless a spirit came with a message I couldn't understand for someone in the audience. That information was personal and only had meaning for the loved ones. Often the person would start crying. It took me years to realize that these individuals weren't crying from sadness, but rather from the love they were receiving from their friends and family on the Other Side.

I enjoyed doing ESP demonstrations. People often laughed and teased one another because of something I'd said. Through the constant challenge of trying to read my audiences, my intuition got stronger, and I began to see and hear the spirits more clearly.

As my psychic accuracy grew and expanded, so did my medical intuition. I began to believe that everyone needed to trust his or her intuition more. Then people would be healthier, feel safer, and live happier lives.

Working with Paul

Paul was a kind, gentle, intelligent man who became my main spiritual mentor. His sense of humor and his memory helped guide me through many scary experiences. He was also very tall, which made my neck hurt when I looked up to talk to him. He asked me to give intuitive readings in his bookstore and the idea of working in his quiet place instead of the noisy restaurant sounded wonderful. In the restaurant, clients decided on the spur of the moment to have a session with me. Paul, on the other hand, insisted that people make appointments.

I had one client who was obstinate about her physician divorcing his wife for her. She had taken his kindness as eternal love. They never met outside of the office, nor had he ever kissed her. I saw that he was happy with his wife and told my client that she was mistaken.

My client began to yell at me. "You're wrong. He loves *me*."

Every sense in my body told me she was wrong. I went to discuss the dilemma with Paul. After hearing my story, he said, "You've just had another growth opportunity. What did you learn?"

"To trust my instincts whether a client agreed or disagreed with my intuitive messages," I answered.

"You got it!"

After a while, Paul asked me to colead his weekly meditation class. While my weekly study group gave me a supportive environment in which to share personal stories and experiment with my intuition, Paul's meditation class was less personal and more academic. He preferred to discuss the history of faith healing, famous healers, and channeling. Paul would often talk about a chapter of a book he'd read. Immediately afterward, I would create a meditation for the group based on the material. My mind was open and so was my active imagination.

Paul kept me level-headed with his humor and common sense. I was shocked when he said to me, "You have only one frontier of fear left—that of the trance experience. I believe you need to complete that level to be a great intuitive."

The only séances I'd ever attended were boring. The channelers either spoke too slowly, didn't always make sense, or had nothing to say that I couldn't read faster. On the other side, I also wondered, wasn't channeling a way for evil to enter a person's mind and take over? Why would I want to become a medium and channel spirits?

I couldn't think of any response to Paul and for months, I pondered these questions. A year later I confronted him. "How would trance work help me overcome my fears?"

"Your fear of trance channeling is limiting your psychic work. Channeling is natural and is more than going into a deep trance. Channeling is a way to tap in to your higher consciousness, to heal, and be healed. It's knowing when it's the right time to take action or knowing who is calling when the phone rings even though it's someone you haven't heard from in years.

"Channeling opens your mind to new ideas, inventions, and creative writing. Once you've conquered this fear, you'll be able to trust your intuition totally. Trance will help you gain additional insights into higher levels of communications. You'll still be in charge of the information and how to deliver it, and your fears of losing control will be gone. Nothing bad will happen to you. I'll help and keep you from harm. You have a sensible mind, you're practical, with a lot of common sense. I wouldn't advise you to delve deeper into trance if you didn't have such a healthy mind You won't draw an evil or destructive spirit. But if one should come, I'll help you get rid of it."

I thought about what he had said; it made sense.

When the Student Is Ready, the Teacher Appears

Marilyn Rosner, a reknowned Canadian medium, was teaching channeling at Paul's Spiritual Advisory Council (SAC) conference. Before signing up for the intensive training, I wanted to observe her skills as a medium.

Marilyn's channeling was exciting. She offered insights so fast it boggled my mind. She was different from anyone I'd ever seen. She didn't sit in a chair and breathe heavily. She was a stand-up medium, who channeled a small child named Daisy. She was someone I wanted to learn from.

The next morning I attended her trance workshop along with fifty other people. Marilyn is about 4'9" and always wears dark sunglasses. She is small but mighty. I sat next to my good friend and astrologer Lee Toman, for reassurance.

She was excited; I was apprehensive. Paul sat across the room, next to Marilyn.

Marilyn began the workshop by explaining how channeling worked through inspiration, creative thinking, creative writing, and imagination. It was her incredible way of working with spirits that inspired me to trust the trance experience. She explained that total trance meant trusting a spirit to use your body and mind to channel words that offered proof of life after life. Her commonsense descriptions made her teaching easy to understand.

Marilyn used meditation techniques to guide us into a deeper trance state. Her strong, soft voice was soothing and kind. She reminded us to let the light enter into our minds. Aloud she invited the spirit teachers, also called avatars, and loved ones to give messages. She welcomed all levels of spirits with love and wisdom.

I heard someone channeling a spirit teacher. I opened my eyes and saw Marilyn standing before one of the attendees encouraging her to speak. "We welcome you," she said. "What do you have to tell us?"

I closed my eyes and heard the attendee give a beautiful, loving message. Others began channeling, too. And then I heard my own voice say, "Do not be afraid. You have much work to do. All is in readiness. Trust your heart and mind."

I could see, hear, and know everything going on in the room, but the sense of peace inside me was greater than anything I'd ever experienced before. Never before had I felt so secure, so radiant, so loved.

Marilyn said, "It is time to return to the present. Slowly open your eyes and return to this room."

I didn't think I had gone into deep trance, but when I tried to stand up, my body felt nailed to the floor. Lee helped me stand and get to the bathroom.

I realized that true channeling was the ultimate peace flowing through me abundantly, that I was coming home to the oneness, God, the real person inside me. I slept soundly that night.

The next morning everyone came early, eager to get started. Paul led us into a short relaxation meditation to set the tone of the day. "Channeling isn't something you can do for hours" he said. "It's important to balance your body and mind first. Let's begin by sharing your thoughts and feelings about what happened last night."

"I couldn't sleep last night. I kept wondering if what we did yesterday was real," said the man next to me.

Paul responded quickly. "What is real and what isn't is for you to decide. How did you relate to the experience?"

"When others were speaking what I thought was channeling, I wondered if they were deluding themselves," my neighbor answered.

Paul looked around the room. "How many of you feel the same?" Half of the attendees raised their hands.

"Good," Paul said. "It's important that you challenge the information. Always balance what you hear with common sense. If it doesn't make sense, just hold off from doing anything."

Another attendee raised her hand. "What if it never makes sense?"

"Then forget it. Does everything you do in your waking state make sense?" There was a loud roar of laughter from the attendees. "You may not be channeling, but just think you are. In that case, you may be confusing yourself with illusions rather than reality," said Paul. "Don't push too fast. Just get used to meditating more deeply until you trust the experience."

Another attendee raised her hand. "I didn't get anything. What does that mean?"

Paul laughed. "I watched you last night. You kept opening your eyes to check everyone out. You were afraid to go too deep." The woman blushed.

Robert Ericsson, retired judge and practicing lawyer, also a cofounder and teacher of SAC, explained, "Channeling doesn't have to be done in any special place. You can do it in a group or by yourself, in the early morning or late at night."

"Remember to always protect yourself with the white light and invite only those spirits that are of the light," continued Paul. "Inspirational writing, meditating, visualizing, drawing, inventing, healing, and prayer may all be ways of channeling. It's easy to do, but hard to validate unless you trust yourself.

"Over 50 percent of widows have had messages from their deceased husbands reported one Gallup Poll. Author and Priest, Andrew Greeley, took a poll and discovered that over 47 percent of the people in the United States believed in life after life," finished Paul.

I learned to never ignore a message from the Other Side.

Steps to See What I See

1. Did you ever have a hunch and didn't listen and wished you had?
   - How did you get the hunch? See it? Hear it? Feel it?
   - Why didn't you trust yourself?
   - What would you do differently now?

2. Practice holding photographs of people's friends or relatives.
   - Notice if you feel hot or cold, fearful or peaceful, happy or sad.
   - Close your eyes and visualize the person in the photograph. Do you see a haze around his or her head? What color is the haze?

3. Ask a friend for a question about a future event.
   - Close your eyes and imagine your friend at the event.
   - Sit quietly for a few minutes and then share what you felt, saw, or heard.

Chapter 3

Making the Ghost Connection

Life is a great surprise. I do not see
why death should not be an even
greater one.
—Vladimir Nabokov

Have you ever talked to a confused person? If they died confused, they'll be the same after death. Confused ghosts don't know that they're dead and are lost between worlds. They haunt us, trying to get our attention. They need our help to find their way.

Hauntings

Hauntings, in general, are caused by these confused ghosts. For example, take two people who lived together for years with little outside interests. The man dies and the wife cannot live without him. If she says things repeatedly after his death like, "I can't live without you. How will I survive? I need you," his soul can become earthbound. When she dies, he doesn't know where to go or what to do. In his confusion, he haunts their old home.

A new buyer comes in and decides to hang a picture on the wall. The ghost resists changes and makes the picture fall. The buyer hangs it again and the picture falls again. He moves the picture to a different wall; the same thing happens. The objects in the dining room hutch get moved or broken. The new owner becomes fearful and sells the house.

The next occupant tries to change the house and has the same experience. Now he knows why he got such a good deal from the former owner. The next buyer gets an even better buy. After a few more buyers and sellers, the house gets a reputation of being haunted and no one wants to buy it. The ghost is satisfied, but still confused. He wants to know where his wife has gone.

Until someone understands what is happening, this man will remain earthbound and confused. Years may pass before help comes. Psychics can help ghosts find peace by talking to them, finding out what happened before death, and guiding them to heaven. I will talk more about this in later chapters.

Ectoplasm

"If you've ever been awakened at night to see a fog pouring out of your closet, you may have seen physical ectoplasm, the substance of ghosts," the metaphysical teacher explained at a SAC conference. "Ectoplasm appears like smoke and emanates from dark places like closets because it cannot exist in light. If you don't understand what's happening, it can be terrifying." Ectoplasm! My mind flashed back to when I was fifteen. Now, for the first time, I understood why the two men always disappeared when my father turned the lights on and why no one else saw them but me. I hadn't been hallucinating.

46

As a teenager, I lived two separate lives. During the day I was a happy teenager, who received good grades, played the piano for school activities, and had lots of friends. At night, I'd turn into a quivering, frightened child.

The teacher went on. "Have any of you ever heard or seen something in the night that frightened you? How old were you? Did your family make fun of your fears?"

"Yes! Yes! Yes!" I wanted to scream.

Deeper and Deeper

"Meditation allows the individual to go above and beyond all physical limitations," our leader explained as she guided us into a state of relaxation. "Allow yourself to visualize the past and present of the people in our group. Trust you'll be able to pick up tidbits of information during this fifteen minutes of silence."

After the time had passed, we were guided back by her whispering voice. "It's time to return to the present. Be aware of the sounds in the room and slowly open your eyes. Look around. What do you see?"

One person said, "I see rainbow colors around some of you."

Another member began to sob. "My uncle, who is dead, spoke to me. When I smelled his cigar, I opened my eyes to see who was smoking. I was surprised to discover that no one was. The smell got stronger and I heard my uncle's voice as clearly as if he was standing next to me. He told me he loved me." Her voice cracked as she shook her head from side to side, unable to go on.

"I heard him, too," another person shouted. "I heard him say 'I love you.' I didn't know who he was, but his left arm was missing."

"Oh my God. He'd lost an arm in the war," the woman answered.

Fear and bewilderment showed on our faces. Our leader waited a moment and then spoke softly. "The left brain interprets, the right brain intuits and perceives what the physical dimension is unable to see. It's easy to become addicted to the trance state, but it's more important to retain your mental balance. In the beginning of trance training, do no more than fifteen to twenty minutes for your own well-being."

I often wondered why my study group members, the university research team, and Paul wanted to have ghost visitors. They weren't afraid to see a ghost, but I was. Why weren't they afraid? For years I tried to resist the ghosts, but they kept coming.

Automatic Writing

The following day, I added automatic writing on my computer to my morning program of meditation, recording my dreams, journaling, and prayer. I wanted more input from my Healing Group. I typed, "Dr. John, how do I protect myself from negative ghosts?"

I placed my hands on my computer keys and went into a deeper state of relaxation while my fingers typed. I didn't know what I was writing. When my fingers stopped typing, I opened my eyes and read what I had written:

Dr. John: Fear is the enemy, not other people's negative energy. Faith is the helper. The rest is learning how to use your spirit teachers. You have many helpers in the spirit world ready to help you.

Ari: You have already overcome so many fears. And you did it by trusting others. Now you have to trust yourself and believe that you will have all the assistance you need, whenever you require it.

Adrienne: *Loving the fear makes it easier to release it.*

Dr. Wu: *Ruth, you don't realize how strong you are. Relax and let your spirit teachers take over the hard parts of your readings. When you get a client with a lot of fear, help her or him to understand and know what to do. You are being prepared to be a Medical Intuitive. Someday you'll realize how strong you are."*

Their words made me feel more secure. I wanted to believe them.

Between Worlds

When my ex-husband died suddenly his mother could not accept his death. She became angry and repeatedly said aloud, "Why did you leave me?"

Her son's spirit heard her and was filled with remorse and guilt for causing his mother this much unhappiness. In his confusion, he became earthbound even though his mother never saw him. Because of her lack of spirit knowledge, she caused her son's spirit further confusion and sorrow. Since then, he has been haunting me as well as many of his relatives.

Dr. John explained how this can happen. "Mourners need to mourn, but must realize that the deceased can hear, even though the survivor may not see or hear them, or be aware of their pain. You can make contact by holding a photo of the deceased and trying to recall a fond memory. Believe that you can connect and you will.

"In the beginning you may only feel, smell, or dream about the spirits. They tend to come in the wee hours of the night when you're not busy doing other things.

"When spirits get stuck on the earthly plateau, they become ghosts, haunting people in their efforts to be heard and seen. Some of the feelings haunted survivors have may be due to natural grieving, but periods of sadness, unexplained fears, overwhelming feelings from people, events, excessive bouts of crying, fears of doom, and darkness in their thoughts may be coming from the deceased.

"The survivors may feel an imbalance or a sense of someone they cannot see in the room. The spirits are not happy being stuck in limbo and neither are the survivors. They want to talk to you as much as you want to talk to them. It is vital at this point in time that more people be raised to a greater level of consciousness so that each becomes aware of the work each must do to increase the spiritual energy."

Healing Work

Healing work is the gift of bringing love, understanding, and closure. The ghost must take three steps down from heaven, whereas the survivor lifts his or herself spiritually three steps up to make the communication. I can either channel the ghost—if our energies are compatible—or talk to the ghost and tell the survivor what I hear. Then I give them the opportunity to talk to each other directly or through me. The conversations often include regrets, love messages, and reassurances that the ghost is all right.

Once everyone has spoken and all has been forgiven, I help them to let go and let God take it from there. The ghost crosses the bridge between worlds and fades into the light of heaven. The survivor fills his or her body with light and love. All are healed.

My ghost healing work began on an international scale when I was asked to speak to a group of widows and widowers at a local church. Before we got started, I asked their president if the group had any common needs. He told me that most of their discussions revolved around the following three questions:

1. Why did our spouses have to die?
2. Why couldn't they overcome their diseases?
3. Is it possible to communicate with our loved ones in spirit?

"Guilt plays a big part in our emptiness, our loneliness, our wish to make up for the past," he said. "Can you deliver a workshop that will help answer these questions?"

I nodded with tears in my eyes and said, "I'll try."
My goals for the evening were to:

1. explain what happens to people after they die,
2. lead a guided meditation to help the attendees make a spirit connection,
3. relieve the stress of the loss of a spouse, and
4. discover why the widows and widowers survived.

Cheryl Lavin, a syndicated reporter covered the event. I thought I might be mentioned briefly in an article, but when the October 31, 1990 edition of the *Chicago Tribune* devoted half of the front page and half of an interior page of the Tempo section to the event, I was surprised and delighted.

The article began, "Put away the crystal ball, the incense, and the gypsy garb—today's 'intuitive counselor' wears a tailored business suit and visits with support groups to summon the spirits of the dead.

"They're all meditating. Or at least they're trying. Except for the one woman who keeps opening her eyes and looking around to see if the others are really going along with this weird stuff. They're trying to contact the dead.

"'The spirits are here. I see them,' says Ruth Berger. 'They have some wonderful messages for us. They want to talk to us.'"

The article was printed throughout the United States and Canada and afterward I received hundreds of phone calls.

Eternal Love

The following Halloween, *Copley News Service* released a follow-up news release on the *Tribune* article to 1,200 radio shows. Following this announcement, I appeared on fifty-five radio shows in one month.

The radio hosts focused on one aspect in the story. "Was sex really better after death?" they wanted to know. Over and over, widows would pull me aside and tell me the same story. "I woke up to my husband lying next to me. It felt so real, I forgot he had died. Our lovemaking went beyond anything we'd ever done before. We didn't get tired or fall asleep. It was incredible! It never happened again, but that convinced me that love is eternal."

Love in the Afterlife

After death, a ghost is freed from the daily concerns of going to work, interacting with other people, and dealing with sickness and can often view the past and present with less emotional pain and more love.

My kind, eighty-six-year-old father-in-law, Sam, was a small-bodied man who always smiled and listened patiently to us. Five years earlier, he had accepted me into the family the same way birds accept the morning sun. Now he was dying and we all knew it.

I'm not sure how long I'd stood by Sam searching his face for a sign of consciousness before I became aware of Kayla's spirit at the foot of the bed. She had died forty years earlier and Sam had never remarried.

Her face was incredibly beautiful, but it was her serenity that gave me peace. She gazed upon Sam and I could hear her loving words in my head. "Do not be afraid. I'll help you when you're ready. Then we'll never be apart again."

Sam had been lying still, resembling a cadaver except for his shallow breathing. But as her words were said, he sat up and extended his arms as if to embrace her. The physical effort was too much for him. He fell back and his forehead broke out in small beads of sweat. He opened his eyes and stared at Kayla.

I thought about all the horror stories we've all heard about the "grim reaper" coming for people's souls. Kayla wasn't a dark, ugly vision, but the person who Sam had loved the most.

Observing Sam and Kayla was like being privy to a special love scene. They weren't aware of me, only of one another. Their love energy expanded until I felt a part of them. They were two ordinary people who had loved each other unconditionally. They didn't touch. They didn't need to.

I thought Sam was ready to die. He'd known for a long time that his health was failing. I wondered if he had been in communication with his beloved wife? Did he know she would be waiting to help him make the transition?

Sam was like many people who had lived to their eighties. He had a healthy respect for longevity. He accepted life and whatever it dealt him. He died the way he lived—quietly and peacefully. No big bang; just a gentle sigh as his body stopped breathing.

I thought about all the people I'd met who didn't have

this kind of love relationship. Who did they reconnect with? What about their enemies? Do they also appear at the end?

Auras at the Time of Death

"Paul, just before my father-in-law died, I saw his aura frayed and lifting away. I'd never seen anything like that before. What does that mean?" I asked my mentor.

"When someone has been ill a long time, their aura becomes weakened, and holes begin to form, like a piece of clothing that's been washed too often. A healthy aura is dense, bright, and close to the head," he explained. "When the soul is ready to let go of the physical body, the soul lifts away approximately twenty-four hours before the actual death. The soul doesn't experience physical death, only observes it. The aura of the person hovers near the body for three days. During that time, the survivors will often feel the presence of the departed."

"I remembered sending my ex-husband into the light sixty-five times after his death, only to have him pulled back by his mother and new wife who wouldn't let him go," I said. "They didn't see or hear him so he kept coming to me."

"When souls become earthbound, they may haunt their former home or find another that is available. You were available," answered Paul.

"That explains why I couldn't get rid of my ex-husband after he died."

"The aura does not die, only transforms into another form of energy. The mental aura and the soul are intertwined," said Paul. "Edgar Cayce, the most famous psychic in the United States, once turned away in horror when he couldn't see the auras of a group of people in an elevator. Immediately after the doors closed, the elevator malfunctioned and killed everyone in it."

Steps to See What I See

1. Have you ever smelled, seen, or felt someone on the other side? Did you feel he or she had a message for you?

2. When you do automatic writing:

   - Always protect yourself by imagining white light enfolding your mind and body.
   - Mentally affirm that only those of the light may enter your meditation.
   - Allow no one else into your light or your thoughts.
   - Hold a photo of a person in your left hand and focus on it.
   - Surround yourself with prayer while holding a pen over a paper.
   - Try not to think. Just let the writing happen.
   - At first the writing will not be clear.
   - Practice daily.
   - Always end with the words, "Amen" or "It is done."

3. For widows and widowers: while looking lovingly at your spouse's photo, imagine him or her next to you.

   - Ask a yes or no question.
   - Does the answer make sense?
   - Trust yourself.

Chapter 4

Ghost Training for the Survivors of Suicide/Murder Victims

If a man harbors any sort of fear, it percolates through all his thinking, damages his personality, makes him landlord to a ghost.
—Lloyd Douglas

A man is killed and doesn't know he's dead. His girlfriend can't hear him and he's frightened. The movie *Ghost* was an accurate account of what happens to people who die suddenly.

As a medical intuitive and medium, I've spoken with thousands of people, both in this world and the next. I've witnessed spirits solving business problems, offering health advice, and dominating or bullying the survivors.

People who die suddenly often become earthbound spirits or ghosts, because they weren't mentally prepared to die.

Their loved ones weren't ready either and find it difficult, if not impossible, to release them. Their survivors feel confused, guilty, angry, and anxious. Love can trap both the ghosts and their loved ones. The ghosts of sudden deaths are the easiest to connect with for a psychic or a medium because they and their loved ones have unfinished business.

Fear Energy Gets Trapped

After my first radio show, a woman named Joann was waiting at the station to talk to me. She sounded desperate. "I hope you can help me. Every time I walk into my dining room, I feel like someone is in there waiting to hurt me, but there's no one there. I feel fine in the other rooms of my home," she explained. "Am I crazy or do I have a ghost in my home?"

Intuitively I saw something like a movie playing in her aura. "Many years ago, the man who lived in the house next door to you, butchered his wife and then killed himself in the room facing your dining room. The woman died looking toward your dining room window for help. The energies of her fear are locked into that space. You and I must pray for them to release the past and move into the light. Afterward, you'll feel safe in every room of your house."

Joann returned after my radio show one month later. "You were right. I checked the records. Thirty years ago, the man next door killed his wife and then shot himself. I did what you told me to do and feel much better walking into my dining room now. Thank you."

When I appeared on the same radio show a year later, Joann came to see me again. "Ruth," she said, "I don't want to live in my house any longer. I'm not afraid, I just want to move. Will the next family that lives in this house have to suffer, too? I wouldn't want anyone to go through the terrible experiences I had."

How caring this woman was. I answered, "You can move now. The spirits are in heaven and are at peace. Bless you for being concerned."

The ghosts of the murderer and murder victim had been earthbound for over thirty years. The only way they could be at peace was for someone to pray for their release.

If you feel someone you know is hurting in the afterlife, visualize the peron walking out of a dark hallway and into a lighted area.When you "see" him fading into the light, say aloud, "I bless you and release you into God's hands."

Suicides Don't Get Off Easy

Kevin Mathews, Chicago radio host, asked me to do a live spirit rescue on his show. I ask my Healing Group what I should do. Dr. John told me to request the following:

1. The individual should be a person suffering from the recent loss of someone who had committed suicide.

2. The person must bring a photo of the deceased to the station.

3. The individual had to have frequent thoughts and dreams of the deceased.

4. The suicide needed to have occurred in the past three months or less.

5. No commercials were to be played during the fifteen or twenty minutes while the spirit rescue was taking place.

The radio station agreed to each of the requests and I asked my daughter Penny to come to the station as my backup "white light battery." The electronics of a radio show and my own psychic energy would need to be balanced for my own mental and physical well-being. Penny's job was to channel the white light over me throughout the spirit rescue.

The man I met at the radio station the following day met all the above requests. He was heavyset, 6'5", with light blue eyes, blond hair. He was also shaking like a leaf about to be blown off a tree.

"Three months ago, my fiancée killed herself by starting the motor of her car in a closed garage. She cuffed her hands to the steering wheel so she could not turn off the motor. The police said she must have changed her mind because her wrists were bruised from the handcuffs," he said.

"She didn't leave a note. I feel so guilty. I see her all the time. I dream about her. Sometimes I want to kill myself too. I can't live without her. What did I do wrong?"

My heart ached for this twenty-three-year-old man. He was like a small child crying out for his mother who had died.

"Can we sit?" I asked. "My neck is getting stiff from trying to look up at you."

He smiled for the first time and said, "Sure."

Once seated, I held his hand and said, "I don't know what happened and I won't know until I connect with your fiancée. I need to explain what you can do to help me make the connection. Did you bring your fiancée's photo?"

Dan took the photo out of his jacket pocket and gave it to me. I gazed at the face of a young woman with brown hair and beautiful blue eyes. She seemed too young to die. "When we get into the radio booth, you're to sit directly opposite me, knees touching. Your knees will be a lot higher than mine. And don't worry."

This time he didn't smile.

"Don't be afraid," I said picking up his thoughts. "This isn't going to hurt and before you leave today, you'll feel a lot better. Once I tune in to your fiancée's vibrations, I'm going to let her use my voice to talk to you. Try to ask her questions that only require a yes or no. She may be too emotional to say more.

"You may feel hot or cold during this part," I continued. "Don't think you're getting sick. It's what happens when the spirit and the earthly world connect. Whatever happens, don't leave. Promise you won't."

"I promise," he said. We were ready.

Kevin Matthews and his cohost invited us into the studio where the event was to take place. The young man sat opposite me as directed and Penny sat a few feet behind me.

Kevin explained to the audience the circumstances of how the young man called to be a part of this experience and how his fiancée had taken her life. "Now Ruth will attempt to connect with the spirit of the deceased to perform a spirit rescue," Kevin told his listeners.

"I am holding the photo of a young woman who took her life, sitting opposite me is her fiancé. I can feel her spirit clearly and strongly. She wants to talk. I am going to let her use my vocal cords to make the connection."

I closed my eyes and prayed, "Dear God. Surround us with white light to fill our thoughts and bodies with thy love and wisdom. Give us the strength to do this healing work."

No sooner had I given the prayer, than I felt the woman's spirit saying, "Forgive me. Forgive me." My voice changed. She was speaking directly through my vocal cords.

"I took my life because I cheated on you who never cheated on me. I couldn't tell you. You were so honest. Please forgive me," said the spirit through me.

"I'm sorry," said Dan.

"You didn't do anything wrong. I'm the bad one."

Dan replied quickly, "You're not. If only you'd have told me, I would have forgiven you. I forgive you now."

My body shivered from the cold. I was freezing. Whenever a spirit used my body, my temperature dropped. I wanted to ask for the heat to be turned up, but I had to help the young woman find peace.

"Listen to my words and then repeat after me," I told Dan. "'I'm going to help you find peace.'"

He repeated my words.

"'Let go and turn around.' Say the words."

Dan was crying. "I don't want to let her go."

"You must. She's in pain. You and I have to help her. She'll come back later when she's healed. You must let her go for now. Tell her you love her and want to help her."

To his credit, he said, "I love you and will always love you, but you have to go now. Later we'll come back together."

"Tell her to turn around and look for the light." He repeated the words.

Clairvoyantly I saw his fiancée turn around and walk toward the light. Nearby was the bridge she had to walk across from this side to the other. "Cross the bridge," I said and he repeated my words.

I saw the spirit "paramedics" coming to escort her into the light. "I let go and let God take her from here," I said.

Dan repeated the words so quietly I could barely hear him.

"Now bring your focus back onto your body. Visualize the light filling your body and when it's complete say aloud, "'It is done.'"

A moment passed before he said, "It is done."

"Bless you for all the good work you did. May you go forth with renewal and joy. Bless you," I finished.

I opened my eyes and saw a miracle. Dan was beaming. "I saw and heard her. Will she be okay now? Will I?" he asked.

"Yes." He hugged me hard.

"But why am I so hot? I thought I was going to burn up with the heat," he asked.

"Excessive heat means you were getting a healing. That's how it works. Feel my hands." He looked bewildered.

"Your hands are like ice. How could you be so cold when I'm so hot?"

"Spirit is cold because spirits don't have a human form," I explained.

Kevin Matthew said in an amazed voice, "I got so hot, I turned up the air conditioning."

People called the radio show reporting feeling too hot or too cold during the spirit rescue. One reason for the extreme cold was that a spirit was trying to talk to them. Excessive heat in their bodies could symbolize a healing was taking place. Many healings took place that day.

What really happens to a person's soul after they die?

How long can they stay here?

Where do they go afterward?

Dr. John had told me, "The more you work with spirits, the more you'll understand and be able to help others." I was beginning to see that he was right.

Letting Go of Loved Ones

I learned that suicides and other sudden deaths don't automatically release the deceased from the mental anguish of their physical lives. The individual who committed suicide is stuck between two worlds. Some people call this level the middle world. Sometimes people who die of natural causes have the same problem.

Letting go seems to be the hardest part for ghosts. Husbands who took care of their wives are reluctant to leave them lest they become easy prey. Wives worry about who will take care of their family members. In the name of love, each can find reasons not to let go. Neither realizes how much they are hurting each other.

If the survivor keeps calling the spirit, the departed soul may feel guilty or responsible for the survivor's problems. In an effort to solve them, a spirit can get stuck between the two worlds.

I remember seeing my ex-husband more after his death than when we were married. His mother and second wife kept pulling him back. They wouldn't let him go. The more this happened, the deeper the women went into depression, and they eventually lost their desire for change in their lives.

If you keep a child from walking, you'd be harming her or his ability to grow and expand. When you hold on to the past, you hurt and limit yourself. The spirit feels your pain and feels awful because there's nothing he or she can do about it. That's the worst pain of all—the feeling of helplessness, of being unable to do anything for the person you love.

Unless the survivors let go, the spirits cannot pave the way to help the newly departed. Just as a parent would be close by for a sick child, the spirits wait patiently for the newly deceased to go with them.

Newly deceased souls are led to a bridge separating the earthly world from the astral world. Crossing the bridge means letting go for now. Once they've crossed over, spirit doctors aid them to sleep, rest, and get well. Since there are no telephones, clocks, or calendars, time is no longer a part of their awareness.

Suicides Can Be Contagious

Two teenagers committed suicide by tying their shoelaces to railroad tracks and dying in each other's arms like Romeo and Juliet.

Dr. John explained, "A double suicide isn't hard to understand when the two love each other. One absorbs the other's thoughts, creating a heightened desire for suicide."

A few weeks later, another double suicide occurred on a train track a few miles away from the first suicide. The second double suicide occurred because of the first couple's negative energies surrounding them. Suicide spirits continue to roam the earthly level, never freeing themselves from the past. The spirits attach themselves to anyone who lets them.

Recently a young woman told me her mother committed suicide when she was five years old. She'd been having thoughts of wanting to kill herself the same way her mother had. She wanted to know how to stop those thoughts.

The woman was tuned in to her mother's thoughts, which were encouraging her to end her life. I suggested she visualize her mother in the white light and place her into the hands of God. Then her fears would vanish.

What Happens After Suicide?

A beautiful woman with ebony-colored skin came to my office to see me. "My therapist thinks you can discourage me from committing suicide. I want to end my life and see no reason to stay alive. I cannot go on living without the man I love. He's left me for another woman. My career isn't important. I have no reason to go on and I know how I'm going to do it," she announced.

I knew she was committed to this course of action, unless I found the right words, this woman would take her life. I asked Dr. John to come through. He said, "Committing suicide doesn't stop you from being depressed. Just the opposite. Only your body dies, not your mind. You're still stuck with all your emotional pain.

"In the physical world, you can get therapy, and hopefully get better. You can stop thinking by going to a play or talking to a friend. But when you commit suicide, you cannot get away from yourself. People can't hear or see you and you can't undo the damage you left behind. You will suffer more," said Dr. John.

She listened, but I felt she still hadn't changed her mind. I told her the following story.

"Years ago the spirit of a man who had committed suicide came to me in trance. His arms and legs were in heavy chains. He kept screaming, 'Help me. Help me!' He explained he'd taken his life so his wife would get his insurance money to pay all their overdue bills. Instead of feeling better, he was in a state of desperation and pain. He couldn't undo what he'd done. Twenty years later, he was still mourning his fate. He couldn't get away from his thoughts and neither can you."

I prayed the woman would not take her life, but feared she would.

Ten years later, she returned. "I thought a lot about what you told me and realized I couldn't stop my pain by killing myself. I hated you for a while. I wanted to die. Your words stopped me.

"Now I'm glad I didn't kill myself. I met a man who gives me unconditional love. My career is flourishing. Thank you for giving me a reason to go on living."

Jewelry Retains a Person's Energy

Jewelry passed on from a loved one can bring the new wearer happiness and peace or pass on negative vibes from suicides, mental illness, or lying. People's energies are often implanted upon the jewelry they wear. If the individual died a sudden, unnatural death, negative impressions may have been implanted in their jewelry and wearing it can hurt you.

My friend Gary introduced me to Shannon, a tall, heavy-set seventeen-year-old. Shannon asked me to tune in to her uncle's watch. The watch burned my hand and flew out to the floor. "You didn't tell me the man who owned this watch was dead," I yelled at Gary.

He winced and said, "I'm sorry. I didn't realize a piece of jewelry from a dead man would affect you this way"

Shannon asked with tears in her eyes, "Can you tell me anything about my uncle? I miss him so."

"Your uncle was suffering from depression. He loved you, but you must stop wearing his watch or you'll get depressed too," I told her.

"I like wearing his watch. It makes me feel closer to him," said Shannon.

My intuition told me her uncle had taken his life and wearing his jewelry was giving this girl similar ideas.

"Put his watch away for now. After he's rested in heaven, you'll be able to put it back on," I said.

She said okay, but I knew she didn't mean it.

Later I asked Gary to tell Shannon's parents that the uncle had committed suicide and was earthbound. Wearing his jewelry could be dangerous to their daughter's emotional well-being.

A few weeks later, my friend called. "Thanks from the parents of Shannon. They'd suspected the death of the uncle was unnatural. They're not going to let Shannon wear any more of her uncle's jewelry." I breathed a sigh of relief.

Do not wear jewelry of a suicide victim. Unknowingly you will begin to feel and think like the deceased. Pack the jewelry up and put it away. Someday you may be able to wear that item without any side effects.

Victims of Murder

"People who die suddenly leave unfinished business," said Dr. John. "They often don't know they're dead and try to communicate through a dense fog. The spirit may only be seen through the third eye or felt through other senses. Novices may smell their loved ones. If the deceased was a good cook, the survivor may smell baking bread, etc. If the deceased smoked cigars, that odor might precede their visit.

"The spirits try to communicate through thought, because they can't see the survivors. That is why the trained medium must say their name aloud—to guide them through the fog," he continued. "Most of the time, the deceased will give helpful information for the living, but not always. The spirit is an extension of the mind. If the mind was in a state of confusion at the time of death, it will continue in the same way."

A Son's Final Message

After the *Tribune* article was published, I began to realize how many people from all walks of life wanted to communicate with loved ones on the other side—college-educated people, white-collar workers, farmers, ministers, lonely people—people who hadn't had a chance to say what they always wanted to.

After my ghost training, I wasn't afraid to do phone consultations any longer. I wanted to serve people and in the process of helping others, I learned more. One of these people was an elderly woman named Millie Browne.

I watched Millie shuffle slowly to the upholstered chair in front of my desk. Her clothes were clean but worn and her nails were raw and broken. Her hands shook as she gave me the photo of her murdered son.

Millie had called out of desperation. "My husband is dead. Now my only child, Ray, was shot twice in the head and left like a bag of garbage behind the hospital where he was a volunteer. It took the police several days to contact me because the murderers took his wallet, his watch, and high school ring. Why was he killed?"

Sobbing, she took the box of tissues I offered and blew her nose. "I never got to say good-bye. Can you help me?"

My heart hurt for this mother as much as if my own child had been killed. If only murderers had to suffer as much as the families of the victims! Why would anyone commit such a horrible crime? And why this woman's son? How would I cope if one of my three children were murdered? The thought was too much and I began to hyperventilate. Stay objective, I commanded my mind. I can't help Millie if I get too emotional. I willed my breathing to slow down.

I love being able to aid survivors to bring closure to their suffering. Often the dead need to say good-bye. Murder, suicide, and sudden deaths cause both sides too much anguish. I tuned in and saw Millie's aura was small and faint, indicating that her energy was far too low.

I gazed at her son's photo. He was a handsome man in his late thirties. He had full lips, with dark skin, and dark brown eyes that held me captive as I traveled back through time. I "saw" that Ray's murder had been swift; he hadn't suffered long. The two men who killed him had no scruples about taking his life.

Moving my right forefinger back and forth over Ray's face in the photo connected me intuitively to him. Slowly, gently, I said aloud what I saw, heard, and felt. "Your son was a good man who helped people whenever he could."

"That was my boy," Millie said.

"Ray wasn't married, and while he didn't live with you, he visited often." A large tear fell onto Millie's jacket leaving a watermark. I prayed silently. "Oh Lord, help me to set them both free to be in thy loving presence."

With eyes closed, I relaxed and began breathing deeper, tuning in to Ray's energies. He'd been a large man, over 250 pounds. I needed to expand my aura to his mammoth energy field. My heartbeat quickened and my head began to hurt. Ray's urgency to make the connection was putting too much pressure on my body.

"Slow down. I need more time to balance our connection," I said to him mentally. He responded immediately and my heart began to beat slower. I silently thanked him.

He said, "You're welcome." I smiled. A polite man.

Millie, unaware of what was occurring, waited quietly while I descended deeper into a trance state. As Ray's energies entered my body, I felt like a balloon being blown up. His energy felt compatible to mine so I gave him permission to use my vocal cords to speak.

"Fight the drug addicts. Don't let them win. They killed me for money for their next fix. Fight them, Ma, with all your might. Don't let them get away. I love you. I'm sorry. I miss you," said Ray through my body. He'd spoken so fast that I didn't have a chance to catch my breath. As if he could read my mind, his voice faded and I felt his energy lift off my body.

With my eyes closed and still in an altered state, I heard my own voice speaking clearly and calmly, "Your son did not die in vain. Go to the corner of your block with your broom, your pots and pans, and tell the gangs to leave. Enlist the help of the other mothers and the gangs will go away. These gang members are the children of the mothers on your block. These women are a mighty force for good. Together they will stop the gangs from meeting and selling drugs on their street."

I "saw" hundreds of mothers marching together to save their children. It was awesome. When I opened my eyes, I saw Millie's shoulders shaking from her silent crying. The mother inside me wanted to cry with her. Would she be able to lead such a group? She was so fragile, so small, so wounded, so lost. She walked out of my office slowly, as if in a daze. My heart broke for her and I hoped that in talking to me I had helped her.

I sat quietly for a long time after Millie left. Drained, I rubbed my forehead and closed my eyes. Death! Why was it so hard for Millie to talk to her son and so easy for me? If I wanted to talk to a loved one in spirit, all I had to do was call.

Six months later, I read that in Millie's neighborhood, the mothers had gone to the corners with the brooms and pans and told the drug pushers to leave—and they had.

Teens and Sudden Death

Sometimes when young people experience a loved one in spirit, they fear that the spirit has come to take them away. A friend of mine called me for help with her teenage daughter, Christie.

"My daughter is hysterical about her friend, Andy, who died recently in a car crash. She says she sees him and is frightened."

"Where is your daughter?" I asked.

"She's right here. I'll put her on."

"Christie, tell me what you're seeing," I said when she came on the phone.

"Ever since I saw Andy in the casket, I've had nightmares about him," she said. "I see him sitting on my friend's couch where he used to like to sit. It scares me. I'm afraid I'll open a door and he'll be standing there."

"What frightens you?"

"That he'll take me with him." Christie's breath was raspy.

"Do you have asthma?"

"No. But lately I've been having a lot of trouble breathing."

"You're stressed out. You need to relax. I can help you. Visualize Andy again, only this time, see him riding a ray of light into the sky. Can you do this?"

"Yes."

"Now visualize yourself on a horse riding swiftly. The sun is shining, the weather is perfect. Soon you and the horse are like one life force riding through fields of grass and flowers."

Christie's labored breathing changed and she began breathing quietly and easily.

"Tell Andy you love him and wish him peace."

After we'd finished I explained, "Andy didn't understand what happened. He came back to you because that's what he always did when he was alive. Don't be afraid. Think love and that will bring both you and Andy peace."

Another teenager, Erica, had a similar experience. I asked her if she ever "felt" her mother after her death.

"Yes, one night I saw a bright light in the doorway when I was thinking about her," Erica said. "I got frightened. I don't want to be afraid anymore."

"Did you know the light represented God?"

"That's why I got so scared. I thought God wanted to take me because I was mean to my mother."

***

Suicide, murder, and sudden death souls get stuck and linger far too long on the earthly side. It is our job—yours and mine—to help these people get help. You wouldn't want to have to sit on a fence for eternity and neither do they.

Ghosts who are stuck on the earthly level can have the mind-set of a frightened six-year-old. You have to take command. Talking to ghosts doesn't mean you're psychotic. You may be hearing voices from the dead because your intuition is asking you to help them. The ghosts of hasty deaths don't understand what has happened. They need your help. Talk to them. They'll answer and then you'll get some sleep.

Steps to See What I See

1. Use the following questions to get in touch with your own intuitive experiences.

    *   Do you know someone who has committed suicide?
    *   Do you feel guilty about this person?
    *   Do you dream about her or him?
    *   Are you afraid?
    *   Are you more depressed than usual?

2. Be aware that people who have died suddenly may need your assistance to go into the light to find peace.

    *   Talk to the spirit and say aloud: "Turn around. Walk to the light. There is someone you know waiting for you." Be firm.
    *   Continue to speak aloud: "It's time for you to find peace. Walk across the bridge where you'll be met by spirit healers who will help you." Again be firm.
    *   Keeping your eyes closed, fill your own body with light until it is completely done. Then say aloud, "It is done."

    Suicides or murder victims may need your help as a group. Do the same as above, but add "ALL of you must go into the light now!" Meditate afterward with prayer and positive thinking to release all negative energies.

3. Find others who want to communicate with loved ones from the Other Side. Don't expect too much at first. Relax and allow the spirit to tell you what still needs to be said. Unless the message is harmful, deliver it as is. If it is a hurtful message, do not say

anything until you've thought about it for twenty-four hours. Be careful what you say.

4. Hold the photo of your loved one and imagine she or he is sitting opposite you.

- Say everything to her or him you ever wanted to say. You can even release your anger, swear, complain, and ask for forgiveness.

- Repeat the above one or more times to get all your feelings out.

- Listen to your loved one.

- Then forgive yourself for everything you did or didn't do for this person. The healing begins when you let go.

5. Check your jewelry for negative energies.

- Select three pieces of similar-sized jewelry and place them on a flat surface.

- Close your eyes and float your left hand back and forth about three inches above the jewelry.

- As your hand moves, note any sensations coming through your hands: coolness, heat, a tingling, or itching. Note whether the sensations are pleasant, comfortable, awful.

- With your eyes still closed, pick up one piece of jewelry and hold it in your left palm. Note if you get more sensations. Put the jewelry down and pick up another piece. Once again, pay attention to whatever you feel. Put the second item down and pick up the third item. Note whatever feelings you experience. You may find that one of these three items will feel different and more pleasant to hold. This is the item you can wear without any negative effect.

Chapter 5

Facts & Myths About Ghosts

*Facts do not cease to exist because
they are ignored.*
—Aldous Huxley

Can our loved ones possess us after they die?
How can I tell if there's a ghost in my home?
Can I contact my deceased mother?

These are some of the many questions I've been getting ever since I was written up as a long-distance exorcist in the best seller, *Ghostly Register,* Contemporary Books, 1986. If the question was general, I'd answer it immediately. If the question was more personal—Do I have a ghost living in my home?—I'd need a photograph of the so-called haunted area to do an assessment.

Intuitively ghosts look, talk, and act just like physical people, except you can see through them. A close friend invited me to a party where a male ghost kept hugging all the women. I could see him, but the others couldn't. He'd float down from the ceiling, land on a woman's lap, and kiss away. He may not have had a physical body, but he still sure was active that night. The others laughed when I told them what the ghost was doing, but none of them saw or sensed him.

Do Ghosts Steal Food?

One of the hundreds of phone calls I've had from people asking about ghosts was from a woman named Mary. She said, "I think a ghost has stolen 100 pounds of potatoes from my garage."

Why would a ghost do that? Ghosts can't cook or eat potatoes.

Then she said, "The same ghost stole a 25-pound rump roast."

"Where was this food kept?" I asked.

"The meat was in the freezer in my garage, next to the potatoes."

"Did you keep the freezer locked?"

"No," she said. "I live in the country. There's no reason to lock my garage."

"Now there is," I said.

The only response I got was the dial tone. A hungry ghost? I don't think so.

Do Ghosts Steal Money?

Brad came to see me about money missing from his wallet. "I get paid on the first and third Saturday of the month, cash my paycheck, pay my bills, and generally have about $100 left in my wallet," he said. "Sometimes when I wake up, there's no money left in my wallet. Do I have a ghost in my bedroom?"

I wondered why a ghost would take money out of his wallet. Where would the ghost spend this cash? On the lottery? A new car? It didn't make sense. Curious, I asked, "Does anyone live with you?"

"Yes, my brother, parents, my sister, and her teenage son."

"Do you drink?"

Sheepishly he grinned." Sometimes I get pretty drunk on the weekend I get paid."

"I don't think you have a ghost, just someone with sticky fingers. Ghosts don't need money. They have nowhere to spend it."

Brad didn't want to believe me. I felt he knew the truth but preferred to believe that a ghost was the thief.

"If you really want to know the truth, I have an idea. Cash your check; keep only what you need and put the balance of your money in a safe deposit box. If you really have a ghost, he or she will be able to bypass the bank security. If nothing is missing, you'll know your thief isn't a ghost," I suggested.

He looked puzzled. He wanted to believe a ghost had taken his money.

Don't assume ghosts steal. Do use your common sense to check out the facts before assuming you have a ghost.

What's Moving My Dining Room Objects?

Julie asked if a ghost was moving the objects in her dining room hutch. She would face her china items forward, only to have them turn around.

"Do you live on a busy traffic street with trucks?"

"Yes, but I don't think that's why my china is turning. I think there's a ghost in my house."

"I don't agree."

She hung up without saying thanks.

Before assuming ghosts are moving your belongings, check your home for physical phenomena that might be causing these occurrences.

Be Careful When Inviting Spirits into Your Home

Virginia was frantic when she called me. "My house lights are blinking on and off. Ever since I used the Ouija board, I've had ghosts waking me up at night moving things around and now my chandelier won't stop twirling. Please help me."

"Using a Ouija board is like calling anyone at all who might be out there. It's an invitation to spirits of people who have died from drugs, alcohol, accidents, murders, and suicides as well as the spirits of your loved ones. Ghosts are earthbound spirits who are stuck between two worlds. Some needed therapy when they were alive and nothing has changed since they died."

My friend John had a similar problem when he called me asking for help for his wife. "I know you're going to admonish me for playing with the Ouija board. I wouldn't have called you, but my wife needs your help.

"Debi and I and another couple were playing with the Ouija board and asked for anyone in the spirit world to make contact with us."

The situation was similar to Virginia's. They had invited ghosts into their homes without knowing the dos and don'ts of channeling. Now they were stuck with ghostly visitors who didn't want to leave.

John continued, "The planchet spelled out answers to our questions. Some were right on and others were way off. We had a good time until Debi began crying. She said she never wanted to participate. I thought it would be fun. I'm sorry now that I talked her into it. The other couple is fine. I'm fine, but my wife isn't. What do I need to do?"

"Put your wife on the phone."

Debi said, "I don't understand. My husband and our friends didn't have this reaction. Why me?"

"Perhaps your emotions were similar to the spirit who entered your body. You might have been frightened and so was the spirit. Like a magnet, you were drawn together. You might also be a spirit healer, but haven't had the proper training to know what to do."

"I don't want to learn anymore," said Debi. "Once this spirit is gone, I'm never going to fool around with anything that has to do with spirits."

Intuitively I knew she'd change her mind later, but for now, a spirit rescue was needed.

"Debi, close your eyes," I told her. "Trust me. I need you to be strong. Ask the spirit what his name is."

"He says Barry."

"Repeat after me. 'Barry, I'm going to help you.'"

Debi said in a shaky voice, "I'm going to help you."

"Say it with conviction."

Boldly Debi repeated, "Barry, I'm going to help you. Trust me. Turn around and look for the light. You'll see someone waiting for you. Tell me who you see."

"It's my mother," Barry said through Debi. "She says I can go home now. I hated her so much. Couldn't stand her rules. I'm sorry for all the rotten things I said and did."

"She forgives you," I told Debi to repeat my words. "Take her hand and cross the bridge."

"I see Barry crossing the bridge," I said. "He'll be fine now. Debi, say a prayer for him and let go of Barry."

Debi followed my instructions. "I feel so much better. Thank you. Will Barry come back?" she asked.

"No. He's gone into the light, but promise you won't play around with the Ouija board again."

"You've got my word."

***

Be careful which spirits you invite into your home. Imagine opening your door on skid row and yelling out into the street, "Come on in. I give all drunks, perverts, murderers, and pimps permission to take over my life and tell me what to do." When you call for "anyone out there," this is what you're doing.

Don't invite just any ghost to come into your home. You might call in a ghost who doesn't want to leave. Once they're your houseguests, they are there to stay. This may even explain some people with multiple personalities. If not helped, these people may begin doing the same things that the dead people did before they died. They may begin to drink more, do weird things, or lose control. But you can get rid of ghosts if you know how.

Put the white light around you whenever you ask someone from the Other Side to contact you and if necessary, tell the ghost to leave in a bold, loud voice.

People Are No Wiser After Death

"Can you contact my husband who's been dead ten years?" asked another woman.

"Why do you want to make contact?"

"I need his help to decide if I should relocate or not."

My intuition said her husband wasn't the right person to ask. "Did your husband give you good advice when he was alive?" I asked gently.

"Heavens no! He wasn't that smart."

"Why do you think he's different now?"

"I thought once people die, they know everything."

***

Spirits don't become any wiser after death and there are no clocks, no calendars, and no daily news in the spirit world.

In other words, don't depend on the spirit keeping up with the market shifts!

Ghosts Live in the Past

When my ex-husband, Dave, died, I was asked to sit in the first car with his second wife and my children on the ride to the cemetery. Dave was sitting on the hearse having a grand time watching people mourn him when he spotted a fast-food restaurant.

"Hey, everyone! Let's stop for a burger." He floated over to the restaurant, but no one went with him. He hadn't let go of his earthly desires yet.

The only one who heard or saw him was me and I don't like fast food. The procession continued on unaware of his request.

Assume ghosts haven't changed.

Bed Bumps in the Night

Penny called me one night at 3:10 A.M., which was most unusual for her. She said, "Linda [her stepmother] and I were talking when the clock chimed ten times but it was 3:00 A.M." Linda told me her clock had never chimed before, in fact it hasn't worked in years. Who or what made the clock chime?"

"How long ago did your father die?"

"Ten years."

"What time of the day did he die?"

"3:00 A.M. Oh my!"

The mystery was solved.

Ghosts Crave Attention

During my daughter Penny's wedding rehearsal, the glass tube in the floral arrangement she was carrying rose up by itself and then fell to the floor and smashed. A second floral arrangement was wedged in the back of the kitchen counter. We watched as the glass tube floated out of the flowers, past the counter, and crashed when it hit the kitchen floor. Penny and I knew intuitively who was causing the breakage.

"We know you're there," I told Dave, her deceased father. "Now stop it."

He wanted to be the center of attention, dead or alive, but he didn't like me yelling at him so he stopped playing pranks.

Never Allow a Ghost to Run Your Life

Searle, one of my students, was still being manipulated by his father, who had died five years previously. "Go to my grave and fix it," his father had demanded at one of our meditation circles.

I suggested Searle make his father's spirit promise not to come back if he did what he wanted this last time. The spirit gave him his word.

When Searle went to the cemetery, he saw his father's grave had sunk twelve inches and was filled with water. Searle had it fixed.

While alive, Searle's father had always controlled him. It wasn't until he was gone completely that Searle was able to meet and marry a wonderful soulmate.

Spirits Can Be Pesky

Mike's father, Jake, had only been dead a short time when he started demanding his son's attention. "It's time for you to pay your bills. Stop what you're doing and do what's important," he would say.

"I can't right now."

"I'm your father. Do what I tell you!"

"Okay."

Jake didn't realize the time and energy necessary for Mike to stop what he was doing to pay his bills. I suggested Mike handle his father differently the next time it happened. Mike was to say, "Thanks for reminding me about the bills. I'll get to it right after I finish this project." If Jake continued insisting, Mike could say, "If you're going to be a nag. I'll stop listening." If he still wouldn't give up, Mike could say, "That's it. I'm closing the curtain. You're out of my space."

Ghosts are pesky and loving ghosts don't always know when to back off. Unless you pay them attention, they'll continue to annoy you in any way they can. Mike had to set limits on his father's spirit—a good way to prevent being haunted. Promise them anything and they'll leave you alone. Don't lose any sleep worrying about the promise.

***

Do people change after death? Don't assume the dead have more power than the living. Do assume the dead will continue to try to control the living.

Spirits Can Be Selfish

A widow called and reported, "I want to remarry, but my dead husband keeps telling me not to. Should I listen to him?"

After contacting her husband in spirit, I said, "Your husband was always a jealous man, wasn't he?"

"Yes."

"He hasn't changed. Just to be sure, check out this new man with your common sense and some background checking," I told her. "If all looks good, go ahead with the marriage."

Steps to See What I See

1. What three new myths about ghosts have you learned?

2. What three facts about ghosts have you learned?

3. Have you had any new ghost experiences since beginning to read this book?

4. Meditate daily with the white light to connect with spirits. Discipline yourself to pick the same time of the day to meditate. If you feel uncomfortable meditating with someone else, don't.

Chapter 6

The Healing Group Answers Our Most Common Questions

*To the dull mind all of nature is
leaden. To the illuminated mind the
whole world sparkles with light.*
— Ralph Waldo Emerson

Reverend Robert Wing, one of my spiritual mentors, said, "For every answer, there are five questions." I had more questions and so did my clients, my study group, and my friends. There was so much more to learn.

How Do I Know If I've Been Cursed?

A client told me the following story about a gypsy fortune-teller who said, "A curse has been put on you. It must be removed. Get a bottle, put three pennies in it, add some water, and place it under your bed for three days. Then I'll exorcise the curse out of your body and mind. My charge will be only $10."

The gypsy fortune-teller kept asking for more money to rid the curse. My client was terrified and paid whatever she asked. During the next six months, my client had given the gypsy over $24,000 in cash, the preferred method of payment.

"The curse is still there," said the gypsy. That's when the woman decided to contact me to get a second opinion.

I explained, "People who believe they're cursed often become victims of crime. They don't see themselves as creators of their circumstances. They seem to have more than their share of negative experiences, the inability to keep a relationship or a job, or they attract one illness after another.

"Perhaps your life was filled with unhappy events beyond the norm. Can those events be explained by logic? Do they defy the common events that happen to all of us? Don't believe you have been cursed again unless you want to give someone more money. Take each experience and analyze it. Your curse may be that you don't believe you can have the life you've dreamed about. Change your mind, change your life."

Since that time, many people have come to me with the same tale of woe. Be careful of people who say a curse has been put on you. Always check these people out. Find out how long they've been doing psychic readings and how long they've been at the address where you met them. Did they ask for a lot of money?

How Do I Open My Mind and Heart?

Helen's father deserted her family when she was a teenager. She never forgave him. When he died, he came back as a spirit to try and heal the past.

Helen came to me for a medical intuitive reading because no one had been able to stop her arthritic pain and stomach ailments. My reading of Helen showed that until she forgave her father, she would continue to suffer. She said, "I will not forgive him. Let him suffer as much as I did." Helen was possessed by her anger. She berated her father for everything that had gone wrong in her life.

I tried to explain but her mind was closed. Knowing I couldn't do any more, I invited my Healing Group to speak to her:

Dr. John: You begin the journey toward wellness of the soul by rising to a higher level of understanding and growing beyond limitations. Accept the God within you. Fear not your power. You have been given spirits who urge you forward to a higher level of healing, peace, and unconditional love for yourself and others.

Adrienne: Love is the force that can catapult you higher. Without love, there is fear. And fear can be the destruction of your body and your thoughts.

Ragu: Training is necessary to direct your energies toward wellness. Anger limits and diminishes your self.

Ari: Courage is the way toward self-trust. Taking a risk, often a small one, such as a change in thinking, increases the flow of natural knowing.

Redman: Nature bends with the wind as you must bend, not break with people you do not agree with. Bodies of water do not stand still and neither can you. You will grow spiritually as you move forward.

Dr. Wu: Laughter raises the body and mind from the lower levels of negativity. Enjoy your journey and expect to be happy. This is good.

Dr. John: All teaching comes from the heart. To learn you must open your heart and mind. It is impossible to learn without these parts open. And so it is. All good comes to those who expect and love. Bless you.

Helen's face was wet from her tears. "How do I open my mind and heart? I don't want to be sick anymore," she asked Dr. John.

"You are accepting that your father was the cause of all your unhappiness. Those thoughts have power over you. This is a form of mental entrapment clouding the truth. You must release your fears and your freedom will restore your mind over false doubts, and restore faith in your own powers.

"Call for your higher self to draw attention away from the physical obstacles. You are never without resources. You seek love but refuse to give prior to payment. Love cannot be bought or sold, only released. Love is a form of energy to be inhaled, as one's body's and soul require. Love cannot be limited to a barter program or its flow will be lessened," Dr. John continued.

"There are many levels of love. There is love a mother feels for her child, love of a man for a woman, and also the love of the Universal Mind, which brings love to every aspect of the soul. Love often comes from forgiveness. Forgive your father for all that he did or didn't do. Then forgive yourself for all the rotten thoughts you had about his leaving. Say it now."

"I don't think I can."

"Just try," said Dr. John through me.

"I forgive my father for everything he did or didn't do. And I forgive me for all the nasty things I said and thought about him," repeated Helen.

"Know that he hears you. Believe. Now say, 'I release you into the hands of God so that you may find peace.'"

At this point Helen was sobbing loudly. Her words came out shaky. "I release you and I release my anger."

Helen had made a major step forward toward healing herself. After our initial session, we'd meet for an hour once a month to meditate, do dream work, and connect with the Healing Group.

Twelve months later, Helen walked into my office radiant. "I've met a man that knew my father. Tom's been telling me stories about how my father taught him to play the drums. He said my father wrote music and donated his free time to play for sick children in hospitals. I'm discovering a lot about my father that I never knew. My mother only talked about his faults.

"Tom's a lot like my father. I don't think we'd have ever met if I was still angry about the past. I've come a long way since our first meeting. Thank you."

How Do We Let Go?

Dr. John: Many souls are entering a state of resistance. These souls seek to grow, but resist that which produces growth. They must allow themselves to feel more without limitations. Repression deters growth and invites anger and disillusionment to fester.

They fear authority figures who demean or corrupt their ideas and create something other than what they intended. These souls must release the fear that others will destroy what they have developed.

Everyone has the opportunity to release negative feelings about others. Some choose to hold on and suffer, whereas others disengage. Know that everyone you encounter is teaching you something. The sooner you learn what that something is, the sooner you will be able to let go. The path of knowledge requires discipline.

Dr. Wu: *These people become so perplexed when they do not understand each has chosen to be born again, to grow and to envision life in a broader manner. Each level of growth requires work and the letting go of past negative habits. They've had many lifetimes and now it is time to manifest the reason for their rebirths. It is the moment for them to expand how they see themselves and their mission.*

Redman: *If these souls would allow more time for physical exercise, they would be able to release pressures and visualize great success. The path of knowledge requires discipline.*

Ari: *Entrapment is of their own making. The mind can be a prison or a beautiful place. When they emerge from their self-imposed imprisonment, they gain clarity and purpose. Then they can see how their spiritual goals can become a reality.*

Adrienne: *People are in great need of offering unconditional love to themselves first so they can give to others without limitations.*

Everything Is Going Well, So Why Do I Feel So Doubtful?

Dr. John: *You are going through a journey, which will take you above the limitations of yourself. Life is a series of lessons to enhance your potential. It is quite common to feel out in space while searching for a means of expression.*

Generally you glide through life while completing lessons, but now you feel stranded in space. You are being forced into your higher thoughts. Learn to observe what is happening without being caught up in the drama.

Redman: *The earth gives and the earth takes. So it is with your thoughts. You are in a time of earth changes.*

What Happens After a Person Dies?

Dr. Wu: *After a person dies, their soul hovers near the body for seventy-two hours. Often the soul gives messages of love and encouragement to the survivors to help them face the future.*

Sudden death souls have more trouble communicating because they may not realize they're dead. On the Other Side spirits are waiting to help them heal emotionally and spiritually. Spirit "paramedics" will take them to a hospital where they can sleep as long as they need to. There are also no bills, and no HMO to tell you when you have to leave. There are no clocks, no calendars, and no demands for your time or expertise.

Then they go to a school where they learn at their own rate, without grade levels, or recesses, and with nothing to get in the way of their learning. They move at their own pace. They don't have to go to work, or drive in traffic, or worry about sickness or crime. They become all mind.

Whenever they awaken, they can visit their family on earth, or view a book in the spirit library, or just go back to sleep. It is a time of transition.

The spirit of a loved one patiently waits at the foot of the bridge between worlds, to help the newly deceased walk across. The bridge is just large enough for one person to walk over a small stream of water.

How Do I Stop Fearing Death?

Imagine a place where you never have to worry about your weight, your health, or growing old, a place where you review your worldly existence and "see" what you've done right or wrong. You will have all the tools and time you need to repair any damage.

In the afterlife, you'll never have to worry if your flight will be delayed. On the Other Side, you can think about someone or something and be there. You decide what you need or want to do next. You can be a guide for either side and develop your soul or just rest.

If everyone could see what I see, there would be no fear of death. Instead there would be joy to reunite with loved ones who have passed on before us.

On the Other Side, there is no crime, no worry about finances or where to live. The only physical pain is in the memories of the past. Concern for the living often overshadows the joy of the peace in the afterlife.

What Is Heaven?

Dr. John: Heaven is a place where people dwell after they've learned their earthly lessons. Heaven is a place in the mind where only thoughts of love exist—love of God, and love of humanity. Heaven is a place where people's souls can review their past lives while contemplating what they will need to learn in their next life. Heaven is a resting space between physical lifetimes.

Adrienne: *Love is the way to heaven. Forgiveness releases the hurts and conflicts of others.*

Ari: *Heaven is a place where you go when your work is done. Work means completion of responsibilities to humanity, to the immediate family, and to the world.*

Redman: *Heaven is the place where good spirits go when they've allowed others to walk beside them.*

Dr. Wu: *Humankind has four levels of thought; self, service, healing, and Godlike thoughts. Each is a form of heaven.*

Ragu: *Heaven allows oneself to walk quietly and effortlessly among other souls who also walk quietly and without inner conflict.*

Heaven is a state of grace.

Am I Making Contact When I Dream About People Who Have Died?

Paul: *Sounds like you are making the connection. Dreams about spirits are generally black and white and are so real, you'll think you're awake. The middle of the night is generally the best time to make the spirit connection.*

Do Angels Exist?

In the beginning of my ghost training I saw spirits who were healers. Later I saw their wings and knew they were angels.

I remember making contact with a fifteen-year-old boy who had died suddenly while playing basketball. The autopsy offered no conclusive evidence for his demise. The family asked me to make contact with the boy to uncover the reason for his death. Jonathan was an excellent student who never took drugs or got into trouble. Yet, he had died suddenly and no one knew why.

Jonathan spoke to his family through me. "Don't be sad. I'm happier than I've ever been. Now I can accomplish more and travel easier. I promise to come back whenever you really need me. It was time for me to go. Don't worry about me. I'm doing God's work. I am at peace."

Jonathan is now an angel.

Why Do Nursing Homes Harbor Spirits?

Often I see groups of spirits laughing, singing, and dancing around the beds of the infirm. The residents in nursing homes are open to seeing and talking to their loved ones in spirit. The spirits are there to demonstrate love, give comfort, and show that death is not the end, but another beginning. The residents travel through time and space to get the training for their next level of learning.

The spirits are visiting the elderly with love.

Why Do We Have a Child Spirit in Our Home?

Redman: The child is searching for a home like the one she lived in before death. When people die suddenly, they dwell in a fog. The only light they see is where love and healers dwell. In your home, the child saw your light and went to it. She found a home like her own.

Why didn't she just go back to her former home?

Redman: She and her parents died in a plane crash. Their light had gone out. She didn't know how to find her way back.

Why Didn't My Best Friend Contact Me After She Died?

> **Ragu:** *Your friend lived an exemplary life. She'd been a nurse and holistic practitioner who did much good while she was alive. She's earned a rest. She will make contact later.*

Can My Aborted Babies Be Haunting Me?

> **Redman:** *Early deaths are lessons for all: the parents, the siblings, the baby. From every experience there is an opportunity to learn. Your baby's early death forced you to analyze your troubled marriage and free yourself.*

How Can I Get a Spirit Guide?

If you want a spirit guide, simply ask for one. Spirits want to help you as much as you want their help.

Judy, a tall, beautiful woman and psychologist, chose to die early rather than get medical help to stop her intestinal pains. Judy, always one to find the humor in life, often pops in to my consultations to offer her insights.

Even though Paul died years ago, he visits whenever I need his help to confirm what's ailing my client.

How Can I Learn More About Ghost Training?

> **Dr. John:** *Invite three or more positive people who wish to develop their channeling skills. If possible, try to meet at least once a week.*
>
> *Meditate for twenty to thirty minutes at each meeting. One person may not develop as rapidly as*

another. Do not become discouraged. What works for someone else may not work for you in the beginning. Support, encouragement, and new ideas all aid in developing your intuitive skills.

Where Are My Loved Ones?

Dr. John: *Read the following and decide for yourself.*

Level 1. The snakepit. Murderers and evil people spend time here. Sometimes individuals who have killed themselves or been under the influence of drugs, alcohol, or mental illness may dwell here until someone helps them go into the light.

Whatever your worst fear is, you will encounter it at this level.

Level 2. The couch potato. Nothing much happens in this level. It's a simple existence, peaceful with hardly any pressure. At this level a person may rest or sleep after a long illness or until the memory of their pain has vanished. They may require a year, ten years, or a hundred years here.

These are the most difficult spirits to contact for the medium, as their memory of pain is too strong for them to communicate with the physical world.

Level 3. The learning level. Here dwell the students, the healers, and the caretakers. They study to understand life. These spirits often are given the opportunity to help those in the physical world.

Level 3 spirits want to gain wisdom and be of service. They study, read books, and learn. Contacting a spirit in level 3 is easier because they want to help.

Level 4. Divinity. Jesus, Mother Theresa, Moses, and the Buddha all dwell in this level of higher good.

Contacting a spirit from level 4 is a joy beyond any physical happiness one can experience. It feels as if you are in the presence of God.

I heard 100 harps playing the first time I saw Jesus in meditation. His blue eyes mesmerized me. Mother Mary came through at the same time. I felt her love and her sacrifice through new eyes. The brightness of their light blinded me and I felt at peace.

Whenever I'm privileged to help others "see" the light, my light is strengthened.

This is the level of saints.

Do Animals See Auras?

"After my father-in-law died, the family German shepherd became vicious and bit right through my leather shoe," I said to Paul.

Paul said, "Spirits need a channel to go through. Sam was using your body to visit his former home. Butch could sense Sam, but not see him. His inability to understand caused him fear. You represented the unknown element and brought out his natural instincts of protection. "Like a small child unwilling to heed his parent's warnings, Butch was caught up in his fears and couldn't get past his emotions."

"I visited a friend whose dog had died recently," I told Paul. "In the past, the cat had often swatted the dog as he walked by the hassock she liked to sit on. The dog would chase the cat, who would run inside the organ opening by the foot pedal.

"I saw the dog's spirit walk by the cat and the cat lift her paw to swipe at the dog. The cat tried to hit the dog and looked confused when she touched empty air. How do you explain this?"

"Spirits of people and animals play very similar games to those of earthly people. Realize that nothing really dies, just sheds the external parts. Inside the mind, things, thoughts, ambitions, dislikes, and loves all appear to remain the same," Paul said.

"I didn't think the cat was having any fun but the dog was enjoying playing a spirit trick."

"You're probably right," he agreed.

Can Animals Get Stuck Too?

A friend and Las Vegas performer asked, "Ruth. Is there a ghost on my foot?"

I looked at his feet and saw the spirit of our wired-haired Dachshund dog. "Don't be afraid. That's our dog, Tupper. She died two years ago. She always liked to sit on people's shoes."

"What's wrong with her?"

"She had asthma before she died."

"Is that why she's breathing so hard?"

"Yes."

"Could you ask her to move? She's scaring me."

"Tupper, come here," I said as I clapped my hands. As she moved closer to me, our friend bid a hasty good night and never returned to our home.

Tupper used to wait for us just inside the front door. We'd often trip on her trying to get past. After she had to be put to sleep, she went back to waiting by the door. She was waiting for her master, my son, to return from the Navy. Only after he returned and she was able to say good-bye, was she able to go to the light.

Steps to See What I See

1. Has anyone ever told you about a curse on you?
   - What did you do about it?
   - Check out the person who told you. Did they ask you for a lot of money in cash to rid the curse? Be wary.

2. Love is the greatest exorcist. Affirm that any thoughts about curses or hexes be transformed into love energy.

3. Have you dreamed about people who have died?
   - Did your dream feel as if you were awake?
   - Was there a message for you or someone else?
   - Did you follow up on the message?

4. If you are in a group, support each other with love and wisdom. Find the good within each other. Outside of the group, the world is often unkind. Sharing a special moment with someone who isn't interested in intuitive training may diminish or hamper your growth.

5. Attend workshops and share what you learn with the group. It will add to the group's knowledge and enhance your communication skills.

6. Read books to further your knowledge.

7. Follow the exercises in chapter 4 to rid your home of hauntings.

Chapter 7

Messages from Spirits

Death begins with life's first breath
and life begins at touch of death.
　　　　　　　　—John Oxenham

My first book, *The Secret Is in the Rainbow,* was about how auras of the people we love can possess our minds and bodies. Spouses get pains similar to the pains of the illness that killed their partners. These "shared" feelings can make it difficult for the survivors to let go, but people in spirit need to get on with their own journey. When loved ones keep them earthbound, all suffer. Here is one story.

She Wanted to Die

"I want to die," said the woman when I answered the phone.

"Who is this?"

"I want to die and I need to know if what you do is against religious teachings."

"It's not. Why are you calling?"

"My son died and I want to die. But I don't want to go against God by talking to you," she said.

"Have we ever met?" I asked. Intuitively I checked her out for a prank and felt her fear. This was a legitimate call, so I didn't hang up. Calmly I asked, "Are you calling me because of the article in the *Chicago Tribune* about my ability to connect people with their loved ones in spirit? I gave that talk in a Catholic Church, so, I don't think your religion would find a problem with you talking to me. Are you calling to ask me to contact your deceased son?"

She gasped. "Can you?"

"There's no guarantee. It's up to the spirit. Can you come to my office and bring a photograph of your son?"

She hung up.

Two days later, she called again. We talked and she didn't hang up, but she didn't make an appointment.

A few days after the second call, she called again to ask if it would be all right if she brought her daughter with her. When the two women arrived, the mother spent the next fifteen minutes going in and out of the bathroom. After her fifth visit to the bathroom, she and her daughter entered my office and sat down.

Holding the photograph of her son made the trance connection easy for me. He told me things I couldn't have known. His mother began to calm down and stopped crying.

She asked, "Why did he die?"

Her son spoke through me. "I'd been sick for so long. I couldn't take it any longer. Please let me go. You keep calling me. Every time I try to stop thinking about you, you make me feel guilty. Please, Mom, let me die in peace."

I asked her permission to let him go. "I don't want him to go," she said.

"He's stuck between the two worlds. That's cruel. You'll be able to talk to him later after he's healed. Let him go."

Sadly she said, "Okay."

Together we helped her son let go and walk into the light.

When she exited my office, she jumped into the air and clicked her heels together like Fred Astaire. She laughed and yelled, "I feel great!"

***

The mother's thoughts of death were not hers, but she didn't know that. She became fearful, depressed, and was unable to give her son the peace that he needed. I could never have done this work without the help of my Healing Group. I saw them surround me with the light and their love before the woman's son used my body to speak through. I thanked them for their help and wise guidance.

First You Have to Believe

Tony wanted to talk to his parents in heaven but didn't believe he was good enough to make the connection. He suffered from a poor self-image. Whenever Tony and I met, his parents in spirit would come along. They loved him very much and wanted to be there to support him.

He sought their approval, which they gave. But he wouldn't accept it because he still felt he was unworthy.

"I wish I could see them like you can," Tony said to me.

"Have faith. Believe," I told him.

"I've tried. I can't," he said.

And so it goes. First you've got to believe. Then you'll see what you want to see.

Her Brother Was Stuck Between Worlds

Leora found her brother, Steve, dead on the toilet in their bi-level home. She lived in the upstairs level, Steve on the lower level. Their dog had always slept downstairs. After Steve's death, Toby would not go downstairs.

Leora consulted me to try and communicate with Steve. Holding Steve's photo, I said, "Your brother is stuck between worlds and you have to help him let go. You wouldn't want to have one leg on the fence and the other leg on the sidewalk. That's how your brother feels right now. Are you willing to let him go so both of you can find peace?"

Copious tears flowed from her eyes. "I can't let go of him. I love him too much."

"That's not love you're feeling. You're afraid. You've got to help send Steve to the light so he can be at peace. Then you won't be so depressed."

She reluctantly agreed to follow my instructions.

Afterward I said, "Steve is fine now, but your home needs to be cleared of the negative energies from his death. The Native Americans used to do a ritual before setting their teepees down. They didn't want to live in any energy field that wasn't their own. You need to purchase a wand of sage. Light the sage and hold it at an angle to get a cloud of smoke pouring forth. It smells like marijuana, so don't be surprised when you use it.

"Take the smoking wand to the basement or lowest level of your home. Go to every corner, closet, wall, stairwell, and bless them individually with the wand saying, 'Bless you. Bless you.'

"Continue on to every level until you've blessed every room in the house. Don't miss the bathrooms or the attic. This will help you sleep better," I finished.

One year later, the woman came back and said, "I did exactly what you said and I feel better. The therapist I was seeing told me how happy he was with my progress. Thank you for all your help."

Does My Mother Have a Message for Me?

"Can you put me in touch with my mother?" asked a client, a well-known radio celebrity. "She died recently and I want to know if she has a message for me."

I held a photo of her mother and noticed her kind eyes. This was a caring, loving, sensitive woman. As I focused on her eyes, I saw the pain in them. "Your mother died of cancer after two years of suffering."

My client nodded, tears flooding her eyes.

"She wants you to know that she is happy and free of pain now. She is grateful for everything you did for her," I told her. "Most of all she wants you to know how proud she is of your accomplishments. She tells me you shouldn't worry about her. She likes where she's at. She met her brother, mother, and father. It's peaceful, just like she thought it would be."

"I wish I could see and hear her."

"You can. Just open yourself up to believing you can. When the time is right, it will happen."

A few months later, my client called and said, "I woke up last night to my mother at the foot of my bed. I could see her clearly, but I was so surprised I got scared and yelled, 'Go away.' As soon as I said go away, she left, and now I want a second chance. Will I get one?"

"Spirits don't want to frighten you, especially someone as loving as your mother was. She might not return for a while, so be patient. Just talk to her as if she was in the room with you. Tell her she's welcome back and this time you won't send her away," I suggested.

Two years later the woman called and said, "I saw her. I saw my mother last night. She came at 2 A.M. You'd told me that spirits like to come between two and four in the morning and you were right. We talked and talked. She said she'll always be there for me. Bless you for all your help."

Son Asks Mother to Leave Husband

"Three years ago my husband had a fight with our sixteen-year-old son, our only child, and kicked him out of our home. He died one week later in a knife fight," said the woman over the phone.

"I feel guilty. I should have never permitted him to kick our son out. Maybe he'd still be alive. Now my husband won't let me talk about our son." Her voice cracked as she sobbed.

"I keep seeing him smacking his fist into his other hand. It was a habit he had whenever he was frustrated. He must be very angry with me. Can you help me?"

Tuning in, I saw her cruel husband beating her over and over. When he was drunk, he felt powerful and enjoyed hurting his wife. "Why do you stay with him?"

She replied, "I have no place to go."

"Let's find out what your son has to tell you," I replied.

Suddenly, out of the phone poured a smoky substance that manifested into a sixteen-year-old teenager smacking his right fist into his left hand. Terrified I asked what he wanted.

"I want my mother to leave my father," he said. "He's going to kill her if she doesn't get away."

Her voice was almost inaudible as she explained, "I'm afraid he'll kill me if I try to leave."

The son yelled, "Go to a shelter. You've got to leave now."

I relayed the message as firmly as I could.

"I'll try," said the woman.

"Now that our session is over, please ask your son to go back the way he came," I pleaded.

"Go back, son. I'll try to leave Dad," she told him.

The boy turned into a cloud of smoke and went back into the telephone. I was badly shaken by this experience. For years I refused to give another phone reading.

Hearing from a Loved One in Spirit Is a Nice Surprise

"It was the weekend of my birthday and all was going well, except for a persistent message to visit my husband's grave," said one of the members of the study group. "My friends had been paying a lot of attention to my birthday and I wasn't particularly thinking of stopping at the gravesite during the weekend, but the message kept playing over and over in my mind. Finally I decided to go to the cemetery five minutes before closing," she continued.

"I stopped at my husband's grave, but nothing happened. Afterward as I started back to my car, I saw something fluttering in the wind. There on the ground just a few feet away from my husband's grave was a banner with two words written on it. The words were 'Happy Birthday.'

"I looked around. Nothing else was close by. No other papers, flowers, or people were near," she said. "The air was still. I knew then the connection between my husband and I would never be over and that he had sent me a very special birthday present."

Infant Talks to Healing Spirit

My two-month-old granddaughter, Dana, was waiting for her mother to finish her chiropractic treatment. I became aware of her cooing to someone on her right.

I tuned in and saw a beautiful dark-haired woman dressed in a long gown of blue-and-gold-colored brocade. Her eyes were large and luminous dark pools of onyx. As if reading my mind, she answered, "I am here to teach Dana metaphysical lessons." Dana cooed louder.

"Does she understand?" I asked the woman.

"Yes," says the beautiful lady. "She has not forgotten her roots."

I smiled.

Her mother always talked to spirits, too. We are now three generations of mediums.

Steps to See What I See

1. Ask for a healing spirit(s) to help you heal others.
   - The spirit may or may not be someone you've known.
   - Imagine the spirit coming from the light and filling you with peaceful thoughts.
   - Ask for the spirit's name.
   - A healing spirit will never demand you do anything harmful to yourself or others.
   - Know that spirits are not aware of your physical body and how tired you may be.
   - Ask the spirit to come back when you are rested.
2. Fear fades as faith begins. Often ghosts send fearful energy when making the connection from their world to ours. Say "I love you," to transform the negative energies.

Chapter 8

Channeling Training

Ghosts only exist for those who
wish to see them.

—Holtei

I've trained thousands of people to make the spirit connection, but not all of them believe they can do it by themselves. They fear being unable to return to their "real world." I understand their concern because I felt the same way once. Ghosts frightened me when they first came knocking. I wanted nothing to do with them even though they always talked to me. In my youth, I was afraid of them and didn't like them. I wanted them to leave me alone but they didn't listen!

Until I found mentors who taught me what I needed to know, I dreaded those nightly visitors. Now I'm not afraid to hear what these "spirits" tell me. Instead, I feel like a joyous child about to enter Disneyworld for the first time. I'm excited for the opportunity to explore a storybook place where I can laugh, see, hear, and feel other dimensions. I know I am protected from harm.

I've learned that when I failed to understand the unknown, it created anxiety in me. I was constantly trying to convert "anxiety unknowns" into comfortable unknowns.

One reason I reached out to others was because I couldn't solve all my problems in isolation. When I went to my spirit group meetings, I could discuss my concerns in safety. I realized I was a spiritual being sharing at a soul level, not simply at an earthly level.

The final frontier of fear meant opening my mind to multiple levels of learning. When children go to grammar school, they have no idea of all they will learn. In the same way earth is only one level of learning, and there is much more.

I learned that many ghosts are fantasy and illusion but may appear real, and that our human capabilities can create things that don't exist except in our minds, some of which is useful, some absolutely destructive. There is no limit to imagination.

Healing takes place within the individual and by the individual. No one can heal anyone else, we can only facilitate the healing process. We have to heal ourselves, to live within a codependency within our environment of emotions and feelings.

From an esoteric view, everyone is created in God's image, which means perfection. Healing in large part comes from understanding our physical, emotional, and intellectual bodies. Eating properly, resting properly, exercising properly, and the like brings us into alignment with our perfection.

In learning to develop new avenues of understanding of self, it is necessary to explore universal truths in keeping with new insights prevalent in our times. Intuitive searching is the natural human connection to the source of all life and creates a personal link to the greater oneness with all of life. The willingness to question is the key to unlocking the spiritual forces within us and to realizing that there is a meaning and purpose to all of life.

Channeling Is Growing

My husband, Dan, and I often hike in the National Parks of the United States and Canada, and both of us are very conscious of the majesty of trees. Each tree had a symbolic message for me. The message might be to reach for the sky, feel the warmth, be aware of how easy change is for nature, how it sleeps in the winter, or generates new growth in the spring.

Once my fears of channeling were behind me, I was reborn as a happier, more successful person. I wanted to rest, to experience rebirth, and be surrounded by others who wanted the same. Life isn't easy, but neither is living in a rut.

If a tree never grew, it would wither and die. Like a tree, I wanted to feel my branches or thoughts growing and expanding. I realized how often people's spirits died with their loved ones, like trees hit by lightning. Life is meant to be lived.

Red Light Channeling

"We're going to do a red light trance session, which can be exciting and scary to a novice," said a SAC instructor. "How many of you have ever been in a trance circle?" Several hands went up. "I need a volunteer," said the instructor. A young man in the audience raised his hand.

"Good," said the teacher. "Please sit in this chair and hold this red bulb attached to a holder just below your chin. The red lamp allows us to observe your face changing or transfiguring into the spirit you are going to attempt to channel. Do not allow the lamp to slip.

Now let's close the shades and shut off all the lights."

As a voice came through the young man, I saw his eyes slant slowly upward as his skin pulled back. He delivered an incredible message of love and healing in an oriental accent.

Excited, I volunteered to be the next subject. Sitting in the chair after the man felt awkward. His energy was different from mine, much bolder and denser. I put the white light on my body to adjust my energy field. I asked the people in the audience to help me by asking for their loved ones to come through. Soon I had a line of spirits waiting to speak.

Each time a spirit came through, I felt their emotions, their needs, and their concerns. People in the audience reported they could see my face change every time a different spirit spoke through me.

I felt pulled from side to side as the spirits pushed and shoved, yelling to be first. They were like children, all trying to be heard. I felt like a football being thrown back and forth. My body hurt afterward.

Paul told me when I shared this experience with him, "You need a gatekeeper, someone to keep the spirits in line."

"How do I get one?" I asked.

"You just ask."

"That simple?"

"Yes. That simple."

The next time I entered into trance, I asked and got a great male gatekeeper who used humor to keep the spirits in line. Since then, my body doesn't hurt after channeling because of the gatekeeper.

Be Careful Who You Study With

One evening, my study group met with another study group at their leader's office. We all sat around a large oval meeting table.

Meditation always gave me peace, but not this night. I felt a dark ominous presence trying to possess me, sucking the breath out of me. I couldn't yell. I couldn't breathe. I thought I was going to die.

My leader saw what was happening and yelled, "Put on the lights! Ruth is in trouble. Open your eyes, Ruth. Look at me."

I was unable to follow her simple command.

"Listen to me. You're all right. You can open your eyes."

I was in a deep, cold, dark place. Her voice sounded far away. She kept repeating the command and finally guided me back into the room.

I was gasping for breath, and my hands shook too hard to hold the glass of water I was told to sip. Thank God my leader had had the presence of mind and the courage to stop the meditation.

I looked around the room and saw the other leader smirking. Intuitively I knew she was the cause of my distress. She had been demonstrating her evil power.

"Ruth, let's leave this room. You can sit in the hallway while we get rid of this mean-spirited ghost." My leader helped me stand on my shaky legs and another member held my arm to steady me.

The other leader and her group left for coffee, but not before she'd invited us to join them.

"We'll see how Ruth feels later," my leader responded.

The door to the meditation room was left open. My group began chanting for the ghost to leave. The chandelier began to twirl. I could feel cold emanating from the room. The lights went on and off as the whirring noise of the chandelier got louder and louder. I saw a dark, ugly mass cry out in the doorway. The chandelier stopped twirling as the mass faded. It was over.

The women came out and said, "It's done, Ruth. You'll be okay now. Let's get out of here."

Still unable to walk by myself, they helped me to my car. We sat for a long time talking. My leader kept rubbing my ice-cold hands until I began to warm up and stop shaking.

"What happened in there?"

She said, "I felt the mean-spirited ghost trying to possess me. I called for my dead father to block it. He stood between it and me and I felt better. I didn't realize it had gone to you until I heard you gasping for air. That's when I yelled, 'Stop.'"

Someone else said, "I sat across the table and heard your voice calling for help. When I opened my eyes, you looked terrified. I didn't know what to do. I was glad when our leader called a halt."

Too Much Trance Work in the Beginning Can Hurt You

I met a woman who did deep trance work twelve hours a day. Her two male spirit teachers told her not to take breaks to go to the bathroom, drink water, or read any books on mediums.

An earlier photo showed her as a beautiful-looking woman. After a few years of doing trance work twelve hours a day, five days a week, she began to grow facial hair and look more like a man. She was convinced that her spirit guides were helping her.

She wasn't listening to her body, or her common sense. Who were these two spirits? After talking with them, I felt they were enjoying the notoriety of their messages and didn't want anything or anyone to stop them. This woman's body was giving her a message that something was wrong. She explained that lately she wasn't feeling good, but her spirits said she was fine and not to worry.

Spirits are not all helpful. They have egos too. They can interrupt your life with their wants and needs. You have to use logic, common sense, and intuition to know if these spirits are mentally healthy or not. Also, spirits don't realize when you've had enough. You have to know when to stop and how to get rid of them.

Don't Ever Touch Someone in Trance

I was deep into meditation during a trance class when the woman next to me said, "Wake up, Ruth. You're missing out."

I was too deep in trance to respond. She shook my shoulder hard and caused me to have a severe headache that lasted for days. Later, I learned that a respected Chicago medium had had a heart attack when someone touched him in deep trance. I was luckier than he was.

The Nature of Spirit Messages

Paul Johnson died and became the seventh spirit guide in my Healing Group. He said, "Psychic messages are generally loving. Psychotic messages are not. Like most human traits, spirit channeling can be good or bad, depending on who is speaking. Like most human gifts, channeling too can be either good or bad, depending on how you use it.

"In today's evolving society, we have many teachers on the spiritual planes offering advice. This information can be useful and inspiring. But each of us needs to question the channeled information to discern if it is right or wrong for us.

"Spiritual contact is the basis of all religious philosophies throughout history. We can tap in to the inner light and live our lives with expanded consciousness.

"Spirits are people who lived on earth just like you and me. They pass over into the spirit world no smarter or wiser than when they were alive. There is no reason to feel they have changed because they have shed their physical bodies. It behooves all to consider the source and judge the material accordingly."

What Do You Believe?

When I was growing up, I thought physical death was the end and that there was no way to conjure up the dead. Now I've learned that no one ever really dies, just the physical body ends and the soul goes on to another level. I know now that it is possible for anyone to communicate with the Other Side.

Paul taught me that during World War II hundreds of cases were reported of wives receiving phone calls from their husbands at the exact time these men were killed in action. The husbands said things like: "Good-bye. I love you. I'll never leave you." The wives felt their husbands in their bedrooms just before sleep or saw them in their dreams.

Imagination? Wishful thinking? Perhaps not! Husbands and wives have a special relationship that surpasses time and space. Physical death isn't the end, only the beginning.

Years later, I realized that it didn't matter how long someone studied or how many books they read. Faith and trust were the major factors to support expanded mind development. I realized that my rapid results were due to the mind training my father had instilled in my brothers and me. "In America, when your mind is open, you can do anything and be anything—if you also work hard," he would tell us. He was right.

I'd been a piano teacher, sales trainer, and retail clothing store manager. I could teach others how to see auras and to trust what they see.

Making Your First Connection

Are you ready to make your connection with the spirit world? Don't hurry. Take time to build your self-confidence. It took me years to overcome my fears of the unknown. Don't worry if you need more time. Ask yourself these questions:

Would you like to make a spirit connection?
Who do you want to contact?
Why do you want to talk to this person?
Do you believe you can communicate?
What do you want to happen?

As you enter into the trance experience, go with a child's imagination. You have many choices. Perhaps you have a loved one who is ill and you want more advice on what to do. You may wish to know if a loved one in spirit is all right or if there is a message for you. Or you may want to meet a spirit teacher, guide, or avatar. All of this is available through the channeling experience.

Your first feeling of a ghost may be a cool breeze over your shoulder. Ghosts don't have a physical body to keep them warm. The anticipation may cause joy, excitement, fear, or some physical reaction such as intestinal upset, a headache, chills, or sweats.

Begin Your Day with Channeling

A great way to begin channeling is to start your day by visualizing a large funnel of light radiating from the sky into every cell of your body and expanding through you into the ground. Keep your mind focused on the light in your body for a full minute to feel grounded and peaceful. Repeat every time you begin to meditate or need a healing.

Meditate five to ten minutes a day before rising, after breakfast, during exercising, or before retiring at night. Anytime is a good time to meditate.

A common complaint I hear is, "I can't keep my mind still long enough to meditate." If you have problems meditating, try these five techniques to aid your concentration:

1. Breathe in a word or phrase such as: "I am at peace," "My mind and body are healthy," "I release all stress," or "All is well." Imagine exhaling your fears.

2. Focusing on how you inhale and exhale will automatically release stress. For example, inhale to four beats and exhale to four beats.

3. Count backward saying the number followed by a calming thought such as, 10. I am relaxed. 9. I am relaxed, and so on.

4. Focus on an aspect of nature such as a tree. Ponder what the tree must feel like to be rooted in the ground and open to the elements. Become the tree.

5. Prayer is talking. Meditation is listening. Ask God to help you find peace.

Begin your meditation with one of the above techniques and soon your mind will lift out of the mundane aspects of life and rise into a higher level of mind consciousness.

Meditation reduces stress and helps you discover how your body and mind coordinate. You'll begin to know when you're really deep when you stop worrying or running a thought over and over in your mind. Meditation, done properly, will refresh and stimulate your mind and body. It will also make it easier to connect with spirits.

The Healing Group's Advice for Effective Channeling

Dr. John: *To be an effective channeler, you must raise your energy three levels above the earthly level so the spirit doesn't have to work so hard. Meditation is the ladder to the master spirit teachers.*

For effective meditation, keep your eyes closed and concentrate on my words. Notice how you're breathing. Try to balance your inhalation with your exhalation. Focus totally on how you are breathing. Is the inhalation as long or as short as the exhalation? Are they smooth or jagged?

Adrienne: *Can you inhale deeply without stress? Say a silent prayer of protection, "I am surrounded by God's light, only good will come to me."*

Imagine a beautiful country scene with a lake surrounded by hills. You can hear the birds singing and children laughing off in the distance. You are at peace.

Visualize a light pouring down from the sky forming a stairway for you to walk on. Coming toward you on the stairway are spirit teachers dressed in long white gowns. One spirit reaches for your hand to guide you to a higher level of consciousness. His loving energies remove all hesitation.

You may feel exhilarated as you release earthly thoughts and limitations. Know your spirit teachers are there to help you.

Dr. John: *Visualize the ladder of light bringing you back into this room. Notice how you're breathing has changed and how calm your body feels.*

When you've gone up three levels, it's much easier to work with your spirit teachers.

Steps to See What I See

1. Support groups with common interests create a safe harbor for learning, and channeling in a group will build your faith. After finding three or more positive thinking people who wish to develop their channeling skills, define your group's intention. Discuss the main purpose of your group. Is it to:

   ◆ make the spirit connection?

   ◆ get psychic messages?

   ◆ get answers to pressing problems?

   ◆ develop intuitive techniques?

   ◆ learn a new way to meditate?

   ◆ tap in to past lives?

   When the group is ready to communicate with the spirit world, your intention might be:

   ◆ to talk to a loved one

   ◆ to get a spirit teacher

   ◆ to heal or receive a healing

   ◆ to have peace of mind

   What you think is what you attract. Take command. Without preplanning, anything can happen and usually does. It is important to set the scene. Support, encouragement, and new ideas all aid in developing the group's ability to connect with spirit.

2. Be in charge of your channeling. You decide how long and who you will channel.

3. Study with a intuitive coach to help uncover intuitive blockages.

4. Read books on metaphysicians to expand your knowledge.

5. Always surround yourself with the light to protect yourself from ghosts who are troubled.

6. Life after life teaches you not to fear death. Learn all you can from the spirits.

7. Remember that ghosts do not keep up with earthly matters. Don't ask them about things they are no longer involved with.

A Final Word

*Our dear ones have passed through
the gateway of the grave into the
endless peace of life eternal. All of us
must inevitably tread the same path,
though we know not when this hour
comes, it shall find us prepared.*
— *Union Prayer Book II for Jewish
Worship*, New York 1962.

I wonder who created this master plan and all its complexities? Why is it that in a world of over two billion people, no two individuals have the same DNA? Incredible! Whoever designed our bodies, our minds, our life styles must have been a superior being.

Death is part of life. To live is to know someone who has died. I remember the hospital chaplain saying, "It will be easier for you to let go of your mother as there is little that can be done to ease her pain."

He was right. When she stopped breathing, I let go.

I've heard people saying to loved ones, "I love you and I give you permission to go to God." I've watched the aura of the sick person lift off as the individual ceases breathing.

I remember a Hollywood movie with actor Edward G. Robinson who was dying while lying on a table listening to his favorite symphonic music and watching movies of all the wonderful times in his life projected on the walls around him. What a wonderful way to make the transition from this world to the next!

In some cultures a dying person sits outside in a special place waiting for his soul to lift off. When it does, the body remains intact. No pain, no suffering, just a releasing of the physical body.

Death is only the beginning.

Author Contact Information

WANTED: Questions and stories about your spiritual experiences that may be used for a future book.

You may contact Ruth Berger for a consultation by phone: 847-390-8084, by Web site: *www.ruthberger.com*, or by letter: Ruth Berger, 701 Forum Sq., Glenview, IL 60025, USA.